TREASURY OF POETRY

TREASURY OF
POETRY

Selected by
Alistair Hedley

Illustrated by
**Kate Aldous, Claire Henley,
Anna Cynthia Leplar, Karen Perrins,
Jane Tattersfield and Sara Walker**

p

This is a Parragon Publishing Book
First published in 2000

Parragon Publishing
Queen Street House
4 Queen Street
Bath BA1 1HE, UK

Created by
The Albion Press Ltd
Spring Hill, Idbury, Oxfordshire OX7 6RU

ISBN 0-75254-179-X

Typeset by York House Typographic, London
Color origination by Classic Scan, Singapore
Printed and bound in Indonesia

CONTENTS

HURT NO LIVING THING and other animal poems 71

THE WORLD and other nature poems   101

THE FAIRIES and other magical poems   131

SIMPLE GIFTS and other poems to make you think   161

THE OWL AND THE PUSSY-CAT
and other story poems   191

HUSH LITTLE BABY and other bedtime poems   221

THERE WAS A NAUGHTY BOY

and

OTHER POEMS OF CHILDHOOD

THERE WAS A NAUGHTY BOY

There was a naughty boy,
A naughty boy was he,
He would not stop at home,
He could not quiet be—
He took
In his knapsack
A book
Full of vowels
And a shirt
With some towels,
A slight cap
For night cap,
A hair brush,
Comb ditto,
New stockings—
For old ones
Would split O!
This knapsack
Tight at's back
He rivetted close
And followed his nose
To the North,

12

To the North,
And followed his nose
To the North.

There was a naughty boy,
And a naughty boy was he,
He ran away to Scotland
The people for to see—
There he found
That the ground
Was as hard,
That a yard

Was as long,
That a song
Was as merry,
That a cherry
Was a red—
That lead
Was as weighty
That fourscore
Was as eighty,
That a door
Was as wooden
As in England—
So he stood in his shoes
And he wondered,
He wondered,
He stood in his shoes
And he wondered.

JOHN KEATS

ALL THE BELLS WERE RINGING

All the bells were ringing,
And all the birds were singing,
When Molly sat down crying
  For her broken doll:
  O you silly Moll!
Sobbing and sighing
  For a broken doll,
When all the bells are ringing
And all the birds are singing.

CHRISTINA ROSSETTI

A GOOD PLAY

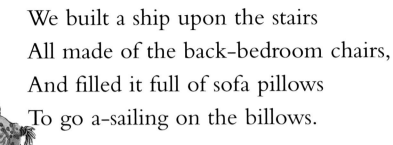

We built a ship upon the stairs
All made of the back-bedroom chairs,
And filled it full of sofa pillows
To go a-sailing on the billows.

We took a saw and several nails,
And water in the nursery pails;
And Tom said, "Let us also take
An apple and a slice of cake";
Which was enough for Tom and me
To go a-sailing on, till tea.

We sailed along for days and days,
And had the very best of plays;
But Tom fell out and hurt his knee,
So there was no one left but me.

ROBERT LOUIS STEVENSON

THE LITTLE DOLL

I once had a sweet little doll, dears,
  The prettiest doll in the world;
Her cheeks were so red and so white, dears,
  And her hair was so charmingly curled.
But I lost my poor little doll, dears,
  As I played in the heath one day;
And I cried for her more than a week, dears;
  But I never could find where she lay.

I found my poor little doll, dears,
  As I played in the heath one day:
Folks say she is terribly changed, dears,
  For her paint is all washed away,
And her arm trodden off by the cows, dears
  And her hair not the least bit curled:
Yet for old sakes' sake she is still, dears,
  The prettiest doll in the world.

CHARLES KINGSLEY

17

MINNIE AND MATTIE

Minnie and Mattie
 And fat little May,
Out in the country,
 Spending a day.

Such a bright day,
 With the sun glowing,
And the trees half in leaf,
 And the grass growing.

Pinky white pigling
 Squeals through his snout,
Woolly white lambkin
 Frisks all about.

Cluck! cluck! the nursing hen
 Summons her folk,—
Ducklings all downy soft,
 Yellow as yolk.

Cluck! cluck! the mother hen
 Summons her chickens
To peck the dainty bits
 Found in her pickings.

Minnie and Mattie
 And May carry posies,
Half of sweet violets,
 Half of primroses.

Give the sun time enough,
   Glowing and glowing,
He'll rouse the roses
   And bring them blowing.

Don't wait for roses
   Losing today,
O Minnie, Mattie,
   And wise little May.

Violets and primroses
   Blossom today
For Minnie and Mattie
   And fat little May.

CHRISTINA ROSSETTI

BROTHER AND SISTER

"Sister, sister go to bed!
Go and rest your weary head."
Thus the prudent brother said.

"Do you want a battered hide,
Or scratches to your face applied?"
Thus his sister calm replied.

"Sister, do not raise my wrath.
I'd make you into mutton broth
As easily as kill a moth!"

The sister raised her beaming eye
And looked on him indignantly
And sternly answered, "Only try!"

Off to the cook he quickly ran.
"Dear Cook, please lend a frying-pan
To me as quickly as you can."

"And wherefore should I lend it you?"
"The reason, Cook, is plain to view.
I wish to make an Irish stew."
"What meat is in that stew to go?"
"My sister'll be the contents!"
                    "Oh!"
"You'll lend the pan to me, Cook?"
                    "No!"

Moral: Never stew your sister.

LEWIS CARROLL

THE SWING

How do you like to go up in a swing,
  Up in the air so blue?
Oh, I do think it the pleasantest thing
  Ever a child can do!

Up in the air and over the wall,
  Till I can see so wide,
Rivers and trees and cattle and all
  Over the countryside—

Till I look down on the garden green,
  Down on the roof so brown—
Up in the air I go flying again,
  Up in the air and down!

ROBERT LOUIS STEVENSON

THE CITY CHILD

Dainty little maiden, whither would you wander?
  Whither from this pretty home, the home where
    mother dwells?
"Far and far away," said the dainty little maiden,
"All among the gardens, auriculas, anemones,
  Roses and lilies and Canterbury-bells."

Dainty little maiden, whither would you wander?
  Whither from this pretty house, this city house
    of ours?
"Far and far away," said the dainty little maiden,
"All among the meadows, the clover and the clematis,
  Daisies and kingcups and honeysuckle-flowers."

ALFRED, LORD TENNYSON

23

A BOY'S SONG

Where the pools are bright and deep,
Where the grey trout lies asleep,
Up the river and o'er the lea,
That's the way for Billy and me.

Where the blackbird sings the latest,
Where the hawthorn blooms the sweetest,
Where the nestlings chirp and flee,
That's the way for Billy and me.

Where the mowers mow the cleanest,
Where the hay lies thick and greenest;
There to trace the homeward bee,
That's the way for Billy and me.

Where the hazel bank is steepest,
Where the shadow falls the deepest,
Where the clustering nuts fall free,
That's the way for Billy and me.

Why the boys should drive away
Little sweet maidens from their play,
Or love the banter and fight so well,
That's the thing I never could tell.

But this I know, I love to play
Through the meadow, among the hay;
Up the water and o'er the lea,
That's the way for Billy and me.

JAMES HOGG

GOING DOWN HILL ON A BICYCLE

With lifted feet, hands still,
I am poised, and down the hill
Dart, with heedful mind;
The air goes by in a wind.

Swifter and yet more swift,
Till the heart with a mighty lift
Makes the lungs laugh, the throat cry:—
"O bird, see; see, bird, I fly.

"Is this, is this your joy?
O bird, then I, though a boy,
For a golden moment share
Your feathery life in air!"

Say, heart, is there aught like this
In a world that is full of bliss?
'Tis more than skating, bound
Steel-shod to the level ground.

Speed slackens now, I float
Awhile in my airy boat;
Till, when the wheels scarce crawl,
My feet to the treadles fall.

Alas, that the longest hill
Must end in a vale; but still,
Who climbs with toil, wheresoe'er,
Shall find wings waiting there.

HENRY CHARLES BEECHING

SKIPPING

Little children skip,
The rope so gaily gripping,
  Tom and Harry,
  Jane and Mary,
  Kate, Diana,
  Susan, Anna,
All are fond of skipping!

The grasshoppers all skip,
The early dewdrop sipping,
  Under, over
  Bent and clover,
  Daisy, sorrel,
  Without quarrel,
All are fond of skipping!

The little boats they skip,
Beside the heavy shipping,
  And while the squalling
  Winds are calling,
  Falling, rising,
  Rising, falling
All are fond of skipping!

The autumn leaves they skip,
When blasts the trees are stripping;
  Bounding, whirling,
  Sweeping, twirling,
  And in wanton
  Mazes curling,
All are fond of skipping!

THOMAS HOOD

29

A CHILD'S LAUGHTER

All the bells of heaven may ring,
All the birds of heaven may sing,
All the wells on earth may spring,
All the winds on earth may bring
　All sweet sounds together;
Sweeter far than all things heard,
Hand of harper, tone of bird,
Sound of woods at sundawn stirred,
Welling water's winsome word,
　Wind in warm wan weather.

One thing yet there is, that none
Hearing ere its chime be done
Knows not well the sweetest one
Heard of man beneath the sun,
　Hoped in heaven hereafter;
Soft and strong and loud and light,
Very sound of very light
Heard from morning's rosiest height,
When the soul of all delight
　Fills a child's clear laughter.

Golden bells of welcome rolled
Never forth such notes, nor told
Hours so blithe in tones so bold,
As the radiant mouth of gold
    Here that rings forth heaven.
If the golden-crested wren
Were a nightingale—why, then,
Something seen and heard of men
Might be half as sweet as when
    Laughs a child of seven.

ALGERNON CHARLES SWINBURNE

THE DUMB SOLDIER

When the grass was closely mown,
Walking on the lawn alone,
In the turf a hole I found
And hid a soldier underground.

Spring and daisies came apace;
Grasses hid my hiding-place;
Grasses run like a green sea
O'er the lawn up to my knee.

Under grass alone he lies,
Looking up with leaden eyes,
Scarlet coat and pointed gun,
To the stars and to the sun.

When the grass is ripe like grain,
When the scythe is stoned again,
When the lawn is shaven clear,
Then my hole shall reappear.

I shall find him, never fear,
I shall find my grenadier;
But, for all that's gone and come,
I shall find my soldier dumb.

He has lived, a little thing,
In the grassy woods of spring;
Done, if he could tell me true,
Just as I should like to do.

He has seen the starry hours
And the springing of the flowers;
And the fairy things that pass
In the forests of the grass.

In the silence he has heard
Talking bee and ladybird,
And the butterfly has flown
O'er him as he lay alone.

Not a word will he disclose,
Not a word of all he knows.
I must lay him on the shelf,
And make up the tale myself.

ROBERT LOUIS STEVENSON

THE CHILDREN'S HOUR

Between the dark and the daylight,
    When the night is beginning to lower,
Comes a pause in the day's occupations,
    That is known as the Children's Hour.

I hear in the chamber above me
    The patter of little feet,
The sound of a door that is opened,
    And voices soft and sweet.

From my study I see in the lamplight,
    Descending the broad hall stair,
Grave Alice, and laughing Allegra,
    And Edith with golden hair.

A whisper, and then a silence:
    Yet I know by their merry eyes
They are plotting and planning together
    To take me by surprise.

A sudden rush from the stairway,
    A sudden raid from the hall!
By three doors left unguarded
    They enter my castle wall!

They climb up into my turret
   O'er the arms and back of my chair;
If I try to escape, they surround me;
   They seem to be everywhere.

They almost devour me with kisses,
   Their arms about me entwine,
Till I think of the Bishop of Bingen
   In his Mouse-Tower on the Rhine!

Do you think, O blue-eyed banditti,
   Because you have scaled the wall,
Such an old mustache as I am
   Is not a match for you all!

I have you fast in my fortress,
   And will not let you depart,
But put you down into the dungeon
   In the round-tower of my heart.

And there will I keep you forever,
   Yes, forever and a day,
Till the walls shall crumble to ruin,
   And moulder in dust away!

HENRY WADSWORTH LONGFELLOW

I REMEMBER, I REMEMBER

I remember, I remember
The house where I was born,
The little window where the sun
Came peeping in at morn;
He never came a wink too soon
Nor brought too long a day;
But now, I often wish the night
Had borne my breath away.

  I remember, I remember
The roses, red and white,
The violets, and the lily-cups—
Those flowers made of light!
The lilacs where the robin built,
And where my brother set
The laburnum on his birthday,—
The tree is living yet!

I remember, I remember
Where I was used to swing,
And thought the air must rush as fresh
To swallows on the wing;
My spirit flew in feathers then
That is so heavy now,
And summer pools could hardly cool
The fever on my brow.

I remember, I remember
The fir trees dark and high;
I used to think their slender tops
Were close against the sky:
It was a childish ignorance,
But now 'tis little joy
To know I'm farther off from Heaven
Than when I was a boy.

THOMAS HOOD

MEET-ON-THE-ROAD

"Now, pray, where are you going?"
  said Meet-on-the Road.
"To school, sir, to school sir,"
  said Child-as-it-Stood.

"What have you in your basket, child?"
  said Meet-on-the-Road.
"My dinner, sir, my dinner, sir,"
  said Child-as-it-Stood.

"What have you for dinner, child?"
  said Meet-on-the-Road.
"Some pudding, sir, some pudding, sir,"
  said Child-as-it-Stood.

"Oh, then I pray, give me a share,"
  said Meet-on-the-Road.
"I've little enough for myself, sir"
  said Child-as-it-Stood.

"What have you got that cloak on for?"
  said Meet-on-the-Road.
"To keep the wind and cold from me,"
  said Child-as-it-Stood.

"I wish the wind would blow through you,"
  said Meet-on-the Road.
"Oh, what a wish! What a wish!"
  said Child-as-it-Stood.

"Pray, what are those bells ringing for?"
  said Meet-on-the Road.
"To ring bad spirits home again,"
  said Child-as-it Stood.

"Oh, then I must be going, child!"
  said Meet-on-the-Road.
"So fare you well, so fare you well,"
  said Child-as-it-Stood.

ANONYMOUS
SCOTTISH

ALONE

From childhood's hour I have not been
As others were,—I have not seen
As others saw,—I could not bring
My passions from a common spring.
From the same source I have not taken
My sorrow; I could not awaken
My heart to joy at the same tone;
And all I loved, I loved alone.
Then—in my childhood—in the dawn
Of a most stormy life was drawn
From every depth of good and ill
The mystery which binds me still:
From the torrent, or the fountain,
From the red cliff of the mountain,
From the sun that round me rolled
In its autumn tint of gold,—
From the lightning in the sky
As it passed me flying by,—
From the thunder and the storm,
And the cloud that took the form
(When the rest of Heaven was blue)
Of a demon in my view.

EDGAR ALLAN POE

THERE WAS AN OLD MAN WITH A BEARD

and

OTHER POEMS ABOUT PEOPLE

THERE WAS AN OLD MAN WITH A BEARD

There was an old Man with a beard,
Who said, "It is just as I feared!—
Two Owls and a Hen, four Larks and a Wren
Have all built their nests in my beard!"

EDWARD LEAR

THERE WAS AN OLD MAN FROM PERU

There was an old man from Peru
Who dreamed he was eating his shoe.
He woke in a fright
In the middle of the night
And found it was perfectly true.

ANONYMOUS
ENGLISH

OZYMANDIAS

I met a traveller from an antique land
Who said: Two vast and trunkless legs of stone
Stand in the desert....Near them, on the sand,
Half sunk, a shattered visage lies, whose frown,
And wrinkled lip, and sneer of cold command,
Tell that its sculptor well those passions read
Which yet survive, stamped on these lifeless things,
The hand that mocked them, and the heart that fed:
And on the pedestal these words appear:
"My name is Ozymandias, king of kings:
Look on my works, ye Mighty, and despair!"
Nothing beside remains. Round the decay
Of that colossal wreck, boundless and bare
The lone and level sands stretch far away.

PERCY BYSSHE SHELLEY

THE STORY OF FLYING ROBERT

When the rain comes tumbling down
In the country or the town.
All good little girls and boys
Stay at home and mind their toys.
Robert thought, "No, when it pours,
It is better out of doors."
Rain it *did*, and in a minute
Bob was in it.
Here you see him, silly fellow,
Underneath his red umbrella.

What a wind! Oh! how it whistles
Through the trees and flowers and thistles!
It has caught his red umbrella;
Now look at him, silly fellow,
Up he flies
To the skies.

No one heard his screams and cries,
Through the clouds the rude wind bore him,
And his hat flew on before him.
Soon they got to such a height,
They were nearly out of sight!
And the hat went up so high
That it really touched the sky.

No one ever yet could tell
Where they stopped or where they fell:
Only, this one thing is plain,
Bob was never seen again!

DR. HEINRICH HOFFMANN

MINNIE AND WINNIE

Minnie and Winnie
  Slept in a shell.
Sleep, little ladies!
  And they slept well.

Pink was the shell within,
  Silver without;
Sounds of the great sea
  Wandered about.

Sleep, little ladies,
  Wake not soon!
Echo on echo
  Dies to the moon.

Two bright stars
    Peeped into the shell.
"What are they dreaming of?
    Who can tell?"

Started a green linnet
    Out of the croft;
Wake, little ladies,
    The sun is aloft!

ALFRED, LORD TENNYSON

MEG MERRILEES

Old Meg she was a Gipsy,
   And lived upon the moors:
Her bed it was the brown heath turf,
   And her house was out of doors.

Her apples were swart blackberries,
   Her currants pods o'broom;
Her wind was dew of the wild white rose,
   Her book a churchyard tomb.

Her Brothers were the craggy hills,
   Her Sisters larchen trees;
Alone with her great family
   She lived as she did please.

No breakfast had she many a morn,
   No dinner many a noon,
And 'stead of supper she would stare
   Full hard against the Moon.

But every morn of woodbine fresh
   She made her garlanding,
And every night the dark glen Yew
   She wove, and she would sing.

And with her fingers, old and brown,
   She plaited Mats o' Rushes,
And gave them to the Cottagers
   She met among the Bushes.

Old Meg was brave as Margaret Queen,
   And tall as Amazon;
An old red blanket cloak she wore;
   A chip hat had she on.
God rest her aged bones somewhere—
   She died full long agone!

JOHN KEATS

AIKEN DRUM

There was a man lived in the moon,
　and his name was Aiken Drum
And he played upon a ladle,
　and his name was Aiken Drum.

And his hat was made of good cream cheese,
　and his name was Aiken Drum.

And his coat was made of good roast beef,
　and his name was Aiken Drum.

And his buttons were made of penny loaves,
　and his name was Aiken Drum.

His waistcoat was made of crust of pies,
　and his name was Aiken Drum.

His breeches were made of haggis bags,
　and his name was Aiken Drum.
And he played upon a ladle,
　and his name was Aiken Drum.

There was a man in another town,
and his name was Willy Wood;
And he played upon a razor,
and his name was Willy Wood.

And he ate up all the good cream cheese,
and his name was Willy Wood.

And he ate up all the good roast beef,
and his name was Willy Wood.

And he ate up all the penny loaves,
and his name was Willy Wood.

And he ate up all the good pie crust,
and his name was Willy Wood.

But he choked upon the haggis bags,
and there was an end of Willy Wood.
And he played upon a razor,
and his name was Willy Wood.

Anonymous
SCOTTISH

THE AKOND OF SWAT

Who or why, or which, or *what,*

        Is the Akond of SWAT?

Is he tall or short, or dark or fair?
Does he sit on a stool or a sofa or chair, or SQUAT,

        The Akond of Swat?

Is he wise or foolish, young or old?
Does he drink his soup and his coffee cold, or HOT,

        The Akond of Swat?

Does he sing or whistle, jabber or talk,
And when riding abroad does he gallop or walk, or TROT,

        The Akond of Swat?

Does he wear a turban, a fez, or a hat?
Does he sleep on a mattress, a bed, or a mat, or a COT,

        The Akond of Swat?

When he writes a copy in round-hand size,
Does he cross his T's and finish his I's with a DOT,

        The Akond of Swat?

Can he write a letter concisely clear
Without a speck or a smudge or smear or BLOT,
The Akond of Swat?

Do his people like him extremely well?
Or do they, whenever they can, rebel, or PLOT,
At the Akond of Swat?

If he catches them then, either old or young,
Does he have them chopped in pieces or hung, or SHOT,
The Akond of Swat?

Do his people prig in the lanes or park,
Or even at times, when days are dark, GAROTTE?
O the Akond of Swat!

Does he study the wants of his own dominion?
Or doesn't he care for public opinion a JOT,
The Akond of Swat?

To amuse his mind do his people show him
Pictures, or any one's last new poem, or WHAT,
For the Akond of Swat?

At night if he suddenly screams and wakes,
Do they bring him only a few small cakes, or a LOT,
      For the Akond of Swat?

Does he live on turnips, tea, or tripe?
Does he like his shawl to be marked with a stripe, or a DOT,
      The Akond of Swat?

Does he like to lie on his back in a boat
Like the lady who lived in that isle remote, SHALLOTT,
      The Akond of Swat?

Is he quiet, or always making a fuss?
Is his steward a Swiss or a Swede or a Russ, or a SCOT,
      The Akond of Swat?

Does he like to sit by the calm blue wave?
Or to sleep and snore in a dark green cave, or a GROTT,
      The Akond of Swat?

Does he drink small beer from a silver jug?

54

Or a bowl? or a glass? or a cup? or a mug? or a POT,

      The Akond of Swat?

Does be beat his wife with a gold-topped pipe,
When she lets the gooseberries grow too ripe, or ROT,

      The Akond of Swat?

Does he wear a white tie when he dines with friends,
And tie it neat in a bow with ends, or a KNOT,

      The Akond of Swat?

Does he like new cream, and hate mince-pies?
When he looks at the sun does he wink his eyes, or NOT,

      The Akond of Swat?

Does he teach his subjects to roast and bake?
Does he sail about on an inland lake, in a YACHT,

      The Akond of Swat?

Some one, or nobody, knows I wot
Who or which or why or what

      Is the Akond of Swat!

EDWARD LEAR

O CAPTAIN! MY CAPTAIN!

O Captain! my Captain! our fearful trip is done,
The ship has weather'd every rack,
   the prize we sought is won,
The port is near, the bells I hear,
   the people all exulting,
While follow eyes the steady keel,
   the vessel grim and daring;
      But O heart! heart! heart!
         O the bleeding drops of red,
            Where on the deck my Captain lies,
               Fallen cold and dead.

O Captain! my Captain! rise up and head the bells;
Rise up—for you the flag is flung—
   for you the bugle trills,
For you bouquets and ribbon'd wreaths—
   for you the shores a-crowding,
For you they call, the swaying mass,
   their eager faces turning;
      Here Captain! dear father!
         This arm beneath your head!
            It is some dream that on the deck,
               You've fallen cold and dead.

My Captain does not answer, his lips are pale and still,

My father does not feel my arm,

  he has no pulse nor will,

The ship is anchor'd safe and sound,

  its voyage closed and done,

From fearful trip the victor ship comes in

  with object won;

    Exult O shores, and ring O bells!

    But I with mournful tread,

      Walk the deck my Captain lies,

      Fallen cold and dead.

WALT WHITMAN

BARBARA FRIETCHIE

Up from the meadows rich with corn,
Clear in the cool September morn,

The clustered spires of Frederick stand
Green-walled by the hills of Maryland.

Round about them orchards sweep,
Apple and peach tree fruited deep,

Fair as the garden of the Lord
To the eyes of the famished rebel horde,

On that pleasant morn of the early fall
When Lee marched over the mountain-wall;

Over the mountains winding down,
Horse and foot, into Frederick town.

Forty flags with their silver stars,
Forty flags with their crimson bars,

Flapped in the morning wind: the sun
Of noon looked down, and saw not one.

Up rose old Barbara Frietchie then,
Bowed with her fourscore years and ten;

Bravest of all in Frederick town,
She took up the flag the men hauled down,

In her attic window the staff she set,
To show that one heart was loyal yet.

Up the street came the rebel tread,
Stonewall Jackson riding ahead.

Under his slouched hat left and right
He glanced; the old flag met his sight.

"Halt!"—the dust-brown ranks stood fast.
"Fire!"—out blazed the rifle blast.

It shivered the window, pane and sash;
It rent the banner with seam and gash.

Quick, as it fell, from the broken staff
Dame Barbara snatched the silken scarf.

59

She leaned far out on the window-sill,
And shook it forth with a royal will.

"Shoot, if you must, this old gray head,
But spare your country's flag," she said.

A shade of sadness, a blush of shame,
Over the face of the leader came;

The nobler nature within him stirred
To life at that woman's deed and word;

"Who touches a hair of yon gray head
Dies like a dog! March on!" he said.

All day long through Frederick street
Sounded the tread of marching feet:

All day long that free flag tost
Over the heads of the rebel host.

Ever its torn folds rose and fell
On the loyal winds that loved it well;

And through the hill-gaps sunset light
Shone over it with a warm good-night.

Barbara Frietchie's work is o'er,
And the Rebel rides on his raids no more.

Peace and order and beauty draw
Round thy symbol of light and law;

And ever the stars above look down
On thy stars below in Frederick town!

Honor to her! and let a tear
Fall, for her sake, on Stonewall's bier.

Over Barbara Frietchie's grave,
Flag of Freedom and Union, wave!

JOHN GREENLEAF WHITTIER

WHEN THAT I WAS AND A LITTLE TINY BOY

When that I was and a little tiny boy,
  With hey, ho, the wind and the rain;
A foolish thing was but a toy,
  For the rain it raineth every day.

But when I came to man's estate,
  With hey, ho, the wind and the rain;
'Gainst knaves and thieves men shut their gate,
  For the rain it raineth every day.

A great while ago the world begun,
  With hey, ho, the wind and the rain;
But that's all one, our play is done,
  And we'll strive to please you every day.

WILLIAM SHAKESPEARE

I EAT MY PEAS WITH HONEY

I eat my peas with honey,
I've done it all my life,
It makes the peas taste funny,
But it keeps them on my knife.

ANONYMOUS
AMERICAN

THREE WISE OLD WOMEN

Three wise old women were they, were they,
Who went to walk on a winter day:
One carried a basket to hold some berries,
One carried a ladder to climb for cherries,
The third, and she was the wisest one,
Carried a fan to keep off the sun.

But they went so far, and they went so fast,
They quite forgot their way at last,
So one of the wise women cried in a fright,
"Suppose we should meet a bear tonight!
Suppose he should eat me!" "And me!!" "And me!!!"
"What is to be done?" cried all the three.

"Dear, dear!" said one, "we'll climb a tree,
There out of the way of the bears we'll be."
But there wasn't a tree for miles around;
They were too frightened to stay on the ground,
So they climbed their ladder up to the top,
And sat there screaming "We'll drop! We'll drop!"

But the wind was strong as wind could be,
And blew their ladder right out to sea;
So the three wise women were all afloat
In a leaky ladder instead of a boat,
And every time the waves rolled in,
Of course the poor things were wet to the skin.

Then they took their basket, the water to bale,
They put up their fan instead of a sail:
But what became of the wise women then,
Whether they ever sailed home again,
Whether they saw any bears, or no,
You must find out, for I don't know.

ELIZABETH T. CORBETT

MY MOTHER

Who fed me from her gentle breast,
And hushed me in her arms to rest,
And on my cheek sweet kisses prest?
      My Mother.

When sleep forsook my open eye,
Who was it sung sweet hushaby,
And rocked me that I should not cry?
      My Mother.

Who sat and watched my infant head,
When sleeping on my cradle bed,
And tears of sweet affection shed?
      My Mother.

When pain and sickness made my cry,
Who gazed upon my heavy eye,
And wept, for fear that I should die?

> My Mother.

Who dressed my doll in clothes so gay,
And fondly taught me how to play,
And minded all I have to say?

> My Mother.

Who ran to help me when I fell,
And would some pretty story tell,
Or kiss the place to make it well?

> My Mother.

Who taught my infant lips to pray,
And love God's holy book and day,
And walk in wisdom's pleasant way?
                              My Mother.

And can I ever cease to be
Affectionate and kind to thee,
Who was so very kind to me,
                              My Mother?

Ah no! the thought I cannot bear,
And if God please my life to spare,
I hope I shall reward thy care,
                              My Mother.

When thou are feeble, old, and grey,
My healthy arm shall be thy stay,
And I will soothe thy pains away,
                    My Mother.

And when I see thee hang thy head,
'Twill be my turn to watch thy bed,
And tears of sweet affection shed,
                    My Mother.

For could our Father in the skies
Look down with pleased or loving eyes,
If ever I could dare despise
                    My Mother?

ANN TAYLOR

ABOU BEN ADHEM

Abou Ben Adhem (may his tribe increase!)
Awoke one night from a deep dream of peace,
And saw, within the moonlight in his room,
Making it rich, and like a lily in bloom,
An angel writing in a book of gold:—
Exceeding peace had made Ben Adhem bold,
And to the presence in the room he said,
"What writest thou?"—The vision raided its head,
And with a look made of all sweet accord,
Answered, "The names of those who love the Lord."
"And is mine one?" said Abou. "Nay, not so,"
Replied the angel. Abou spoke more low,
But cheerily still; and said, "I pray thee then,
Write me as one that loves his fellow-men."

   The angel wrote, and vanished. The next night
It came again with a great wakening light,
And showed the names whom love of God had blessed,
And lo! Ben Adhem's name led all the rest.

LEIGH HUNT

HURT NO LIVING THING

and

OTHER ANIMAL POEMS

HURT NO LIVING THING

Hurt no living thing,
  Ladybird nor butterfly,
Nor moth with dusty wing,
Nor cricket chirping cheerily,
Nor grasshopper, so light of leap,
  Nor dancing gnat,
  Nor beetle fat,
Nor harmless worms that creep.

CHRISTINA ROSSETI

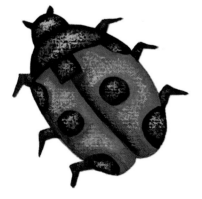

THE COW

The friendly cow all red and white,
   I love with all my heart:
She gives me cream with all her might,
   To eat with apple tart.

She wanders lowing here and there,
   And yet she cannot stray,
All in the pleasant open air,
   The pleasant light of day;

And blown by all the winds that pass
   And wet with all the showers,
She walks among the meadow grass
   And eats the meadow flowers.

ROBERT LOUIS STEVENSON

THE LAMB

Little lamb, who made thee?
Dost thou know who made thee?
Gave thee life, and bid thee feed
By the stream and o'er the mead;
Gave thee clothing of delight,
Softest clothing, woolly, bright;
Gave thee such a tender voice,
Making all the vales rejoice?
Little lamb, who made thee?
Dost thou know who made thee?

Little lamb, I'll tell thee,
Little lamb, I'll tell thee:
He is callèd by thy name,
For he calls himself a lamb.
He is meek, and he is mild;
He became a little child.
I a child, and thou a lamb,
We are callèd by his name.
Little lamb, God bless thee!
Little lamb, God bless thee!

WILLIAM BLAKE

75

TO A BUTTERFLY

I've watched you now a full half-hour,
Self-poised upon that yellow flower;
And, little Butterfly! indeed
I know not if you sleep or feed.
How motionless!—not frozen seas
More motionless! And then
What joy awaits you, when the breeze
Hath found you out among the trees,
And calls you forth again!

This plot of orchard-ground is ours;
My trees they are, my Sister's flowers.
Here rest your wings when they are weary;
Here lodge as in a sanctuary!
Come often to us, fear no wrong;
Sit near us on the bough!
We'll talk of sunshine and of song,
And summer days, when we were young;
Sweet childish days, that were as long
As twenty days are now.

WILLIAM WORDSWORTH

CATERPILLAR

Brown and furry
Caterpillar in a hurry,
Take your walk
To the shady leaf, or stalk,
Or what not,
Which may be the chosen spot.
No toad spy you,
Hovering bird of prey pass by you;
Spin and die,
To live again a butterfly.

CHRISTINA ROSSETTI

THE FIELDMOUSE

Where the acorn tumbles down,
  There the ash tree sheds its berry,
With your fur so soft and brown,
  With your eye so round and merry,
Scarcely moving the long grass,
Fieldmouse, I can see you pass.

Little thing, in what dark den,
  Lie you all the winter sleeping?
Till warm weather comes again,
  Then once more I see you peeping
Round about the tall tree roots,
Nibbling at their fallen fruits.

Fieldmouse, fieldmouse, do not go,
  Where the farmer stacks his treasure,
Find the nut that falls below,
  Eat the acorn at your pleasure,
But you must not steal the grain
He has stacked with so much pain.

Make your hole where mosses spring,
  Underneath the tall oak's shadow,
Pretty, quiet, harmless thing,
  Play about the sunny meadow.
Keep away from corn and house,
None will harm you, little mouse.

CECIL FRANCES ALEXANDER

THE FLY

Little Fly,
Thy summer's play
My thoughtless hand
Has brushed away.

Am not I
A fly like thee?
Or art not thou
A man like me?

For I dance,
And drink, and sing,
Till some blind hand
Shall brush my wing.

If thought is life
And strength and breath,
And the want
Of thought is death;

Them am I
A happy fly,
If I live
Or if I die.

WILLIAM BLAKE

80

LADYBIRD! LADYBIRD!

Ladybird! Ladybird! Fly away home,
Night is approaching, and sunset is come:
The herons are flown to their trees by the Hall;
Felt, but unseen, the damp dewdrops fall.
This is the close of a still summer day;
Ladybird! Ladybird! haste! fly away!

EMILY BRONTË

THE SNAKE

A narrow fellow in the grass
Occasionally rides;
You may have met him, —did you not?
His notice sudden is.

The grass divides as with a comb,
A spotted shaft is seen;
And then it closes at your feet
And opens further on.

He likes a boggy acre,
A floor too cool for corn.
Yet when a child, and barefoot,
I more than once, at morn,

Have passed, I thought, a whip-lash
Unbraiding in the sun,—
When, stooping to secure it,
It wrinkled, and was gone.

Several of nature's people
I know, and they know me;
I feel for them a transport
Of cordiality;

But never met this fellow,
Attended or alone,
Without a tighter breathing,
And zero at the bone.

EMILY DICKINSON

THE TYGER

Tyger! Tyger! burning bright
In the forests of the night,
What immortal hand or eye
Could frame thy fearful symmetry?

In what distant deeps or skies
Burnt the fire of thine eyes?
On what wings dare he aspire?
What the hand dare seize the fire?

And what shoulder, and what art,
Could twist the sinews of thy heart?
And, when thy heart began to beat,
What dread hand? and what dread feet?

What the hammer? what the chain?
In what furnace was thy brain?
What the anvil, what dread grasp
Dare its deadly terrors clasp?

When the stars threw down their spears,
And water'd heaven with their tears,
Did he smile his work to see?
Did he who made the Lamb make thee?

Tyger! Tyger! burning bright
In the forests of the night,
What immortal hand or eye,
Dare frame thy fearful symmetry?

WILLIAM BLAKE

THE CAMEL'S COMPLAINT

Canary-birds feed on sugar and seed,
   Parrots have crackers to crunch;
And as for the poodles, they tell me the noodles
   Have chicken and cream for their lunch.
      But there's never a question
      About *my* digestion—
        Anything does for me.

Cats, you're aware, can repose in a chair,
   Chickens can roost upon rails;
Puppies are able to sleep in a stable,
   And oysters can slumber in pails.
      But no one supposes
      A poor camel dozes—
        Any place does for me.

Lambs are enclosed where it's never exposed,
   Coops are constructed for hens;
Kittens are treated to houses well heated,
   And pigs are protected by pens.
      But a camel comes handy
      Wherever it's sandy—
        Anywhere does for me.

People would laugh if you rode a giraffe,
   Or mounted the back of an ox;
It's nobody's habit to ride on a rabbit,
   Or try to bestraddle a fox.
      But as for a camel, he's
      Ridden by families—
         Any load does for me.

A snake is as round as a hole in the ground,
   And weasels are wavy and sleek;
And no alligator could ever be straighter
   Than lizards that live in a creek.
      But a camel's all lumpy
      And bumpy and humpy—
         Any shape does for me.

CHARLES F. CARRYL

THE KANGAROO

Old Jumpety-Bumpety-Hop-and-Go-One
Was lying asleep on his side in the sun.
This old kangaroo, he was whisking the flies
(With his long glossy tail) from his ears and his eyes.
Jumpety-Bumpety-Hop-and-Go-One
Was lying asleep on his side in the sun,
Jumpety-Bumpety-Hop!

ANONYMOUS
AUSTRALIAN

88

THE EAGLE

He clasps the crag with crooked hands;
Close to the sun in lonely lands,
Ring'd with the azure world, he stands.

The wrinkled sea beneath him crawls;
He watches from his mountain walls,
And like a thunderbolt he falls.

ALFRED, LORD TENNYSON

THE GREAT BROWN OWL

The brown owl sits in the ivy bush,
  And she looketh wondrous wise,
With a horny beak beneath her cowl,
  And a pair of large round eyes.

She sat all day on the selfsame spray,
  From sunrise till sunset;
And the dim, grey light it was all too bright
  For the owl to see in yet.

"Jenny Owlet, Jenny Owlet," said a merry little bird,
  "They say you're wondrous wise;
But I don't think you see, though you're looking at *me*
  With your large, round, shining eyes."

But night came soon, and the pale white moon
  Rolled high up in the skies;
And the great brown owl flew away in her cowl,
  With her large, round, shining eyes.

AUNT EFFIE (JANE EUPHEMIA BROWNE)

THE OWL

When cats run home and light is come,
   And dew is cold upon the ground,
And the far-off stream is dumb,
   And the whirring sail goes round,
   And the whirring sail goes round;
   Alone and warming his five wits,
   The white owl in the belfry sits.

When merry milkmaids click the latch,
   And rarely smells the new-mown hay,
And the cock hath sung beneath the thatch
   Twice or thrice his roundelay,
   Twice or thrice his roundelay;
   Alone and warming his five wits,
   The white owl in the belfry sits.

ALFRED, LORD TENNYSON

91

DUCKS' DITTY

All along the backwater,
Through the rushes tall,
Ducks are a-dabbling.
Up tails all!

Ducks' tails, drakes' tails,
Yellow feet a-quiver,
Yellow bills all out of sight
Busy in the river!

Slushy green undergrowth
Where the roach swim—
Here we keep our larder,
Cool and full and dim.

Every one for what he likes!
We like to be
Heads down, tails up,
Dabbling free!

High in the blue above
Swifts whirl and call—

We are down a-dabbling
Up tails all!

KENNETH GRAHAME

LITTLE TROTTY WAGTAIL

Little Trotty Wagtail, he went in the rain,
And twittering, tottering sideways, he ne'er got
   straight again;
He stooped to get a worm, and looked up to get a fly,
And then he flew away ere his feathers they were dry.

Little Trotty Wagtail, he waddled in the mud,
And left his little footmarks, trample where he would,
He waddled in the water-pudge, and waggle went his tail,
And chirrupped up his wings to dry upon the garden rail.

Little Trotty Wagtail, you nimble all about,
And in the dimpling water-pudge you waddle in and out;
Your home is nigh at hand and in the warm pigsty;
So, little Master Wagtail, I'll bid you a goodbye.

JOHN CLARE

EPIGRAM

*Engraved on the Collar of a Dog which I Gave to His
Royal Highness*

I am his Highness' Dog at Kew:
Pray tell me, sir, whose dog are you?

ALEXANDER POPE

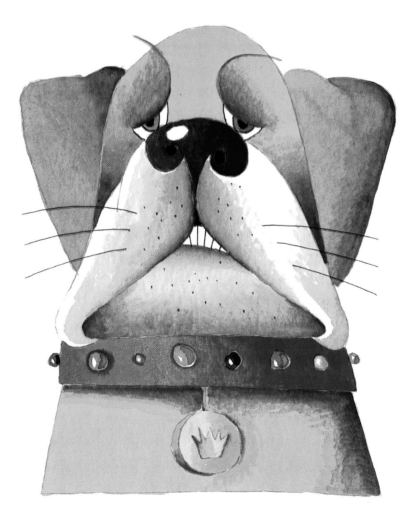

MOTHER TABBYSKINS

Sitting at a window
In her cloak and hat
I saw Mother Tabbyskins,
The *real* old cat!
Very old, very old,
Crumplety and lame;
Teaching kittens how to scold—
Is it not a shame?

Kittens in the garden
Looking in her face,
Learning how to spit and swear—
Oh, what a disgrace!
Very wrong, very wrong,
Very wrong and bad;
Such a subject for our song,
Makes us all too sad.

Old Mother Tabbyskins,
Sticking out her head,
Gave a howl, and then a yowl,
Hobbled off to bed.

Very sick, very sick,
Very savage, too;
Pray send for a doctor quick—
Any one will do!

Doctor Mouse came creeping,
Creeping to her bed;
Lanced her gums and felt her pulse,
Whispered she was dead.
Very sly, very sly,
The *real* old cat
Open kept her weather eye—
Mouse! beware of that!

Old Mother Tabbyskins,
Saying "Serves him right",
Gobbled up the doctor, with
Infinite delight.
Very fast, very fast,
Very pleasant, too—
"What a pity it can't last!
Bring another, do!"

ELIZABETH ANNA HART

97

TWO LITTLE KITTENS

Two little kittens
One stormy night,
Began to quarrel,
And then to fight.

One had a mouse
And the other had none;
And that was the way
The quarrel begun.

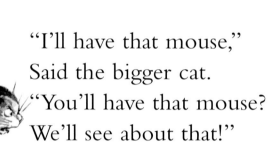

"I'll have that mouse,"
Said the bigger cat.
"You'll have that mouse?
We'll see about that!"

"I will have that mouse,"
Said the tortoise-shell;
And, spitting and scratching,
On her sister she fell.

I've told you before
'Twas a stormy night,
When these two kittens
Began to fight.

The old woman took
The sweeping broom,
And swept them both
Right out of the room.

The ground was covered
With frost and snow,
They had lost the mouse,
And had nowhere to go.

So they lay and shivered
Beside the door,
Till the old woman finished
Sweeping the floor.

And then they crept in
As quiet as mice,
All wet with snow
And as cold as ice.

They found it much better
That stormy night,
To lie by the fire,
Than to quarrel and fight.

JANE TAYLOR

99

THE CAT OF CATS

I am the cat of cats. I am
    The everlasting cat!
Cunning, and old, and sleek as jam,
    The everlasting cat!
I hunt the vermin in the night—
    The everlasting cat!
For I see best without the light—
    The everlasting cat!

WILLIAM BRIGHTY RANDS

THE
WORLD

and

OTHER NATURE POEMS

THE WORLD

Great, wide, beautiful, wonderful World,
With the wonderful water round you curled,
And the wonderful grass upon your breast—
World, you are beautifully dressed.

The wonderful air is over me,
And the wonderful wind is shaking the tree,
It walks on the water, and whirls the mills,
And talks to itself on the tops of the hills.

You friendly Earth, how far do you go,
With the wheatfields that nod and the rivers that flow,
With cities and gardens, and cliffs, and isles,
And people upon you for thousands of miles?

Ah, you are so great, and I am so small,
I tremble to think of you, World, at all;
And yet, when I said my prayers today,
A whisper inside me seemed to say,
"You are more than the Earth, though you are such a dot:
You can love and think, and the Earth cannot."

WILLIAM BRIGHTY RANDS

102

ANSWER TO A CHILD'S QUESTION

Do you ask what the birds say? The sparrow, the dove,
The linnet and thrush say, "I love and I love!"
In the winter they're silent, the wind is so strong;
What it says I don't know, but it sings a loud song.
But green leaves, and blossoms, and sunny warm weather,
And singing and loving—all come back together.
But the lark is so brimful of gladness and love,
The green fields below him, the blue sky above,
That he sings, and he sings, and for ever sings he,
"I love my Love, and my Love loves me."

SAMUEL TAYLOR COLERIDGE

ALL THINGS BRIGHT AND BEAUTIFUL

All things bright and beautiful,
  All creatures great and small,
All things wise and wonderful,
  The Lord God made them all.

Each little flower that opens,
  Each little bird that sings,
He made their glowing colors,
  He made their tiny wings.

The purple-headed mountain,
  The river running by,
The sunset, and the morning,
  That brightens up the sky;

The cold wind in the winter,
  The pleasant summer sun,
The ripe fruits in the garden,
  He made them every one.

He gave us eyes to see them,
  And lips that we might tell,
How great is God Almighty,
  Who has made all things well.

CECIL FRANCES ALEXANDER

THE MONTHS OF THE YEAR

January brings the snow;
Makes the toes and fingers glow.

February brings the rain,
Thaws the frozen ponds again.

March brings breezes loud and shrill,
Stirs the dancing daffodil.

April brings the primrose sweet,
Scatters daisies at our feet.

May brings flocks of pretty lambs,
Skipping by their fleecy dams.

June brings tulips, lilies, roses;
Fills the children's hands with posies.

Hot July brings cooling showers,
Strawberries and gilly-flowers.

August brings the sheaves of corn,
Then the Harvest home is borne.

Warm September brings the fruit,
Sportsmen then begin to shoot.

Fresh October brings the pheasant;
Then to gather nuts is pleasant.

Dull November brings the blast,
Then the leaves are falling fast.

Chill December brings the sleet,
Blazing fire and Christmas treat.

SARA COLERIDGE

SPRING

Sound the Flute!
Now it's mute.
Birds delight
Day and Night;
Nightingale
In the dale,
Lark in Sky,
Merrily,
Merrily, Merrily, to welcome in the Year.

Little Boy,
Full of joy;
Little Girl,
Sweet and small;
Cock does crow,
So do you;
Merry voice,
Infant noise,
Merrily, Merrily, to welcome in the Year.

Little Lamb,
Here I am;
Come and lick
My white neck;
Let me pull
Your soft Wool;
Let me kiss
Your soft face;
Merrily, Merrily, we welcome in the Year.

WILLIAM BLAKE

CHILD'S SONG IN SPRING

The silver birch is a dainty lady,
　　She wears a satin gown;
The elm tree make the old churchyard shady,
　　She will not live in town.

The English oak is a sturdy fellow,
　　He gets he green coat late;
The willow is smart is a suit of yellow,
　　While brown the beech trees wait.

Such a gay green gown God gives the larches—
　　As green as He is good!
The hazels hold up their arms for arches
　　When Spring rides through the wood.

The chestnut's proud and the lilac's pretty,
　　The poplar's gentle and tall,
But the plane tree's kind to the poor dull city—
　　I love him best of all!

E. NESBIT

TO DAFFODILS

Fair daffodils, we weep to see
  You haste away so soon;
As yet the early-rising Sun
  Has not attain'd his noon.
   Stay, stay
  Until the hasting day
   Has run
  But to the even song;
And, having pray'd together, we
  Will go with you along.

We have short time to stay, as you,
  We have as short a Spring;
As quick a growth to meet decay,
  As you, or anything.
   We die
  As your hours do, and dry
   Away
  Like to the Summer's rain;
Or as the pearls of morning's dew,
  Ne'er to be found again.

ROBERT HERRICK

111

THE DAYS ARE CLEAR

The days are clear,
  Day after day,
When April's here
  That leads to May,
And June
Must follow soon:
  Stay, June, stay!—
If only we could stop the moon
And June!

CHRISTINA ROSETTI

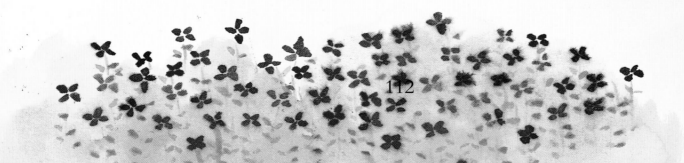

112

AUTUMN FIRES

In the other gardens
    And all up the vale,
From the autumn bonfires
    See the smoke trail!

Pleasant summer over
    And all the summer flowers,
The red fire blazes,
    The grey smoke towers.

Sing a song of seasons!
    Something bright in all!
Flowers in the summer,
    Fires in the fall!

ROBERT LOUIS STEVENSON

SNOW

In the gloom of whiteness,
In the great silence of snow,
A child was sighing
And bitterly saying: "Oh,
They have killed a white bird up there on her nest,
The down is fluttering from her breast!"
And still it fell through that dusky brightness
On the child crying for the bird of the snow.

EDWARD THOMAS

WINTER

When icicles hang by the wall,
  And Dick the shepherd blows his nail,
And Tom bears logs into the hall,
  And milk comes frozen home in pail;
When blood is nipp'd and ways be foul,
Then nightly sings the staring owl,
    To-whit! to-who!
    A merry note,
While greasy Joan doth keel the pot.

When all aloud the wind doth blow,
  And coughing drowns the parson's saw;
And birds sit brooding in the snow,
  And Marian's nose looks red and raw;
When roasted crabs hiss in the bowl,
Then nightly sings the staring owl,
    To-whit! to-who!
    A merry note,
While greasy Joan doth keel the pot.

WILLIAM SHAKESPEARE

THAW

Over the land freckled with show half-thawed
The speculating rooks at their nests cawed
And saw from elm-tops, delicate as flower of grass,
What we below could not see, winter pass.

EDWARD THOMAS

WEATHERS

This is the weather the cuckoo likes,
  And so do I;
When showers betumble the chestnut spikes,
  And nestlings fly;
And the little brown nightingale bills his best,
And they sit outside at "The Travellers' Rest,"
And maids come forth sprig-muslin drest,
And citizens dream of the south and west,
  And so do I.

This is the weather the shepherd shuns.
  And so do I;
When beeches drip in browns and duns,
  And thresh, and ply;
And hill-hid tides throb, throe on throe,
And meadow rivulets overflow,
And drops on gate-bars hang in a row,
And rooks in families homeward go,
  And so do I.

THOMAS HARDY

BLOW, BLOW, THOU WINTER WIND

Blow, blow, thou Winter wind,
Thou art not so unkind
  As man's ingratitude;
Thy tooth is not so keen,
Because thou art not seen,
  Although thy breath be rude.
Heigh ho! sing heigh ho! unto the green holly;
Most friendship is feigning, most loving mere folly:
  Then heigh ho, the holly!
  This life is most jolly.

Freeze, freeze, thou bitter sky,
Thou dost not bite so nigh
  As benefits forgot;
Though thou the waters warp,
Thy sting is not so sharp
  As friend remembered not.
Heigh ho! sing heigh ho! unto the green holly;
Most friendship is feigning, most loving mere folly:
  Then heigh ho, the holly!
  This life is most jolly.

WILLIAM SHAKESPEARE

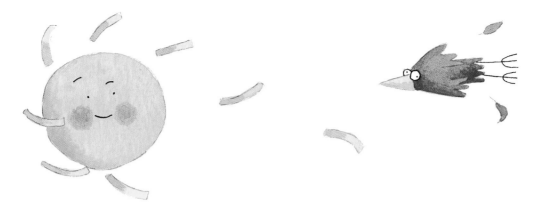

LITTLE WIND

Little wind blow on the hilltop;
Little wind, blow down the plain;
Little wind, blow up the sunshine,
Little wind, blow off the rain.

KATE GREENAWAY

THE WIND AND THE MOON

Said the Wind to the Moon, "I will blow you out;
    You stare
    In the air
    Like a ghost in a chair,
Always looking what I am about—
I hate to be watched; I'll blow you out."

The Wind blew hard, and out went the Moon.
    So deep
    On a heap
    Of clouds to sleep,
Down lay the Wind, and slumbered soon,
Muttering low, "I've done for that Moon."

He turned in his bed; she was there again!
    On high
    In the sky,
    With her one ghost eye,
The Moon shone white and alive and plain.
Said the Wind, "I will blow you out again."

The Wind he took to his revels once more;

On down,

In town,

Like a merry-mad clown,

He leaped and hallooed with whistle and roar—

"What's that?" the glimmering thread once more!

He flew in a rage—he danced and blew;

But in vain

Was the pain

Of his bursting brain;

For still the broader the Moon-scrap grew,

The broader he swelled his big cheeks and blew.

Slowly she grew—till she filled night,

And shone

On her throne

In the sky alone,

A matchless, wonderful silvery light,

Radiant and lovely, the queen of the night.

The Wind blew hard, and the Moon grew dim.
  "With my sledge
  And my wedge,
  I have knocked off her edge!
If only I blow right fierce and grim,
The creature will soon be dimmer than dim."

He blew and he blew, and she thinned to a thread,
  "One puff
  More's enough
  To blow her to snuff!
One good puff more where the last was bred,
And glimmer, glimmer, glum will go the thread."

He blew a great blast, and the thread was gone.
  In the air
  Nowhere
  Was a moonbeam bare;
Far off and harmless the shy stars shone—
Sure and certain the Moon was gone!

Said the wind: "What a marvel of power am I!
        With my breath,
        God faith!
        I blew her to death—
First blew her away right out of the sky—
Then blew her in; what strength have I!"

But the Moon she knew nothing about the affair;
        For high
        In the sky,
        With her one white eye,
Motionless, miles above the air,
She had never heard the great Wind blare.

GEORGE MACDONALD

BREAD AND MILK FOR BREAKFAST

Bread and milk for breakfast,
  And woollen frocks to wear,
  And a crumb for robin redbreast
  On the cold days of the year.

CHRISTINA ROSSETTI

WINDY NIGHTS

Whenever the moon and stars are set,
   Whenever the wind is high,
All night long in the dark and wet,
   A man goes riding by
Late in the night when the fires are out,
Why does he gallop and gallop about?

Whenever the trees are crying aloud,
   And ships are tossed at sea,
By, on the highway, low and loud,
   By at the gallop goes he.
But at the gallop he goes, and then
By he comes back at the gallop again.

ROBERT LOUIS STEVENSON

ADDRESS TO A CHILD DURING A BOISTEROUS WINTER EVENING

What way does the Wind come? What way does he go?

He rides over the water, and over the snow,

Through wood, and through vale; and o'er rocky height,

Which the goat cannot climb, takes his sounding flight;

He tosses about in every bare tree,

As, if you look up, you plainly may see;

But how he will come, and whither he goes,

There's never a scholar in England knows.

He will suddenly stop in a cunning nook,
And rings a sharp 'larum; but, if you should look,
There's nothing to see but a cushion of snow
Round as a pillow, and whiter than milk,
And softer than if it were covered with silk.
Sometimes he'll hide in the cave of a rock,
Then whistle as shrill as the buzzard cock.
Yet seek him—and what shall you find in his place?
Nothing but silence and empty space;
Save, in a corner, a heap of dry leaves,
That he's left, for a bed, to beggars or thieves!

As soon as 'tis daylight, tomorrow with me
You shall go to the orchard, and then you will see
That he has been there, and made a great rout,
And cracked the branches, and strewn them about:
Heaven grant that he spare but that one upright twig
That looked up at the sky so proud and big
All last summer, as well you know,
Studded with apples, a beautiful show!

Hark! over the roof he makes a pause,
And growls as it he would fix his claws
Right in the slates, and with a huge rattle
Drive them down, like men in a battle.
But let him range round; he does us no harm,
We build up the fire, we're snug and warm;
Untouched by his breath, see the candle shines bright,
And burns with a clear and steady light.
Books have we to read—but that half-stifled knell,
Alas! 'tis the sound of the eight o'clock bell.

Come, now we'll to bed! and when we are there
He may work his own will, and what shall we care?
He may knock at the door—we'll not let him in;
May drive at the windows—we'll laugh at his din.
Let him seek his own home, wherever it be:
Here's a cosy warm house for Edward and me.

DOROTHY WORDSWORTH

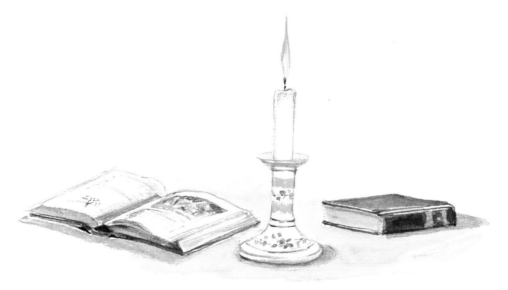

HAPPY THOUGHT

The world is so full of a number of things,
I'm sure we should all be as happy as kings.

ROBERT LOUIS STEVENSON

THE FAIRIES

and

OTHER MAGICAL
POEMS

THE FAIRIES

Up the airy mountain,
  Down the rushy glen,
We daren't go a-hunting
  For fear of little men;
Wee folk, good folk,
  Trooping all together;
Green jacket, red cap,
  And white owl's feather!

Down along the rocky shore
  Some make their home;
They live on crispy pancakes
  Of yellow tide-foam;
Some in the reeds
  Of the black mountain lake,
With frogs for their watch-dogs,
  All night awake.

High on the hill-top
  The old King sits;
He is now so old and grey
  He's nigh lost his wits.
With a bridge of white mist

Columbkill he crosses,
On his stately journeys
  From Slieveleague to Rosses;
Or going up with music
  On cold starry nights,
To sup with the Queen
  Of the gay Northern Lights.

They stole little Bridget
  For seven years long;
When she came down again,
  Her friends were all gone.
They took her lightly back,
  Between the night and morrow,
They thought that she was fast asleep,
  But she was dead with sorrow.
They have kept her ever since
  Deep within the lake,
On a bed of flag-leaves,
  Watching till she wake.

By the craggy hill-side,
  Through the mosses bare,
They have planted thorn-trees
  For pleasure here and there.

Is any man so daring
  As dig them up in spite,
He shall find the thornies set
  In his bed at night.

Up the airy mountain,
  Down the rushy glen,
We daren't go a-hunting
  For fear of little men;
Wee folk, good folk,
  Trooping all together;
Green jacket, red cap,
  And white owl's feather!

WILLIAM ALLINGHAM

THE BELLS

Hear the sledges with the bells—
    Silver bells!
What a world of merriment their melody foretells!
    How they tinkle, tinkle, tinkle,
      In the icy air of night!
    While the stars that oversprinkle
    All the heavens, seem to twinkle
      With a crystalline delight;
    Keeping time, time, time,
    In a sort of Runic rhyme,
To the tintinnabulation that so musically wells
    From the bells, bells, bells, bells,
      Bells, bells, bells—
From the jingling and the tinkling of the bells.

EDGAR ALLAN POE

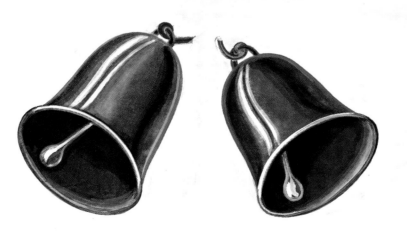

135

THE MAD GARDENER'S SONG

He thought he saw an Elephant,
   That practised on a fife;
He looked again, and found it was
   A letter from his wife.
"At length I realize," he said,
   "The bitterness of Life!"

He thought he saw a Buffalo
   Upon the chimney-piece:
He looked again, and found it was
   His Sister's Husband's Niece.
"Unless you leave this house," he said,
   "I'll send for the Police!"

He thought he saw a Rattlesnake
   That questioned him in Greek:
He looked again, and found it was
   The Middle of Next Week.
"The one thing I regret," he said,
   "Is that it cannot speak!"

He thought he saw a Banker's Clerk
  Descending from the bus:
He looked again, and found it was
  A Hippopotamus:
"If this should stay to dine," he said,
  "There won't be much for us!"

He thought he saw a Kangaroo
  That worked a coffee-mill:
He looked again, and found it was
  A Vegetable-Pill.
"Were I to swallow this," he said,
  "I should be very ill!"

He thought he saw a Coach-and-Four
  That stood beside his bed:
He looked again, and found it was
  A Bear without a Head.
"Poor thing," he said, "poor silly thing!
  It's waiting to be fed!"

He thought he saw an Albatross
　That fluttered round the lamp:
He looked again, and found it was
　A Penny-Postage-Stamp.
"You'd best be getting home," he said,
　"The nights are very damp!"

He thought he saw a Garden-Door
　That opened with a key:
He looked again, and found it was
　A Double Rule of Three:
"And all its mystery," he said,
　"Is clear as day to me!"

He thought he saw an Argument
　That proved he was the Pope:
He look again, and found it was
　A Bar of Mottled Soap.
"A fact so dread," he faintly said,
　"Extinguishes all hope!"

LEWIS CARROLL

IF A PIG WORE A WIG

If a pig wore a wig,
  What could we say?
Treat him as a gentleman,
  And say "Good day."

If his tail chanced to fail,
  What could we do?
Send him to the tailoress
  To get one new.

CHRISTINA ROSSETTI

CALICO PIE

Calico Pie,
The little Birds fly
Down to the calico tree,
Their wings were blue,
And they sang "Tilly-loo!"
Till away they flew,—
And they never came back to me!
They never came back!
They never came back!
They never came back to me!

Calico Jam,
The little Fish swam,
Over the syllabub sea,
He took off his hat,
To the Sole and the Sprat,
And the Willeby-wat,—
But he never came back to me!
He never came back!
He never came back!
He never came back to me!

Calico Ban,
The little Mice ran,
To be ready in time for tea,
Flippity flup,
They drank it all up,
And danced in the cup,—
But they never came back to me!
They never came back!
They never came back!
They never came back to me!

Calico Drum,
The Grasshoppers come,
The Butterfly, Beetle, and Bee,
Over the ground,
Around and round,
With a hop and a bound,—
But they never came back!
They never came back!
They never came back!
They never came back to me!

EDWARD LEAR

KUBLA KHAN

In Xanadu did Kubla Khan
　A stately pleasure-dome decree;
Where Alph, the sacred river, ran
Through caverns measureless to man
　Down to a sunless sea.

So twice five miles of fertile ground
With walls and towers were girdled round;
And here were gardens bright with sinuous rills
Where blossomed many an incense-bearing tree;
And here were forests ancient as the hills,
Enfolding sunny spots of greenery.

But O, that deep romantic chasm which slanted
Down the green hill athwart a cedarn cover!

A savage place! as holy and enchanted
As e'er beneath a waning moon was haunted
By woman wailing for her demon-lover!
And from this chasm, with ceaseless turmoil seething,
As if this earth in fast thick pants were breathing,
A mighty fountain momently was forced;
Amid whose swift half-intermitted burst
Huge fragments vaulted like rebounding hail,
Or chaffy grain beneath the thresher's flail:
And 'mid these dancing rocks at once and ever:
It flung up momently the sacred river.
Five miles meandering with a mazy motion
Through wood and dale the sacred river ran,
Then reached the caverns measureless to man,
And sank in tumult to a lifeless ocean:
And 'mid this tumult Kubla heard from far
Ancestral voices prophesying war!

The shadow of the dome of pleasure
Floated midway on the waves;
Where was heard the mingled measure
From the fountain and the caves.
It was a miracle of rare device,
A sunny pleasure-dome with caves of ice!
A damsel with a dulcimer
In a vision once I saw:
It was an Abyssinian maid,
And on her dulcimer she played,
Singing of Mount Abora.
Could I revive within me
Her symphony and song,
To such a deep delight 'twould win me,
That with music loud and long,
I would build that dome in air,
That sunny dome! those caves of ice!
And all who heard should see them there,
And all should cry, Beware! Beware!
His flashing eyes, his floating hair!
Weave a circle round him thrice,
And close your eyes with holy dread,
For he on honey-dew hath fed,
And drunk the milk of Paradise.

SAMUEL TAYLOR COLERIDGE

144

WHERE LIES THE LAND

Where lies the land to which the ship would go?
Far, far ahead, is all her seamen know.
And where the land she travels from? Away,
Far, far behind, is all that they can say.

On sunny noons upon the deck's smooth face,
Linked arm in arm, how pleasant here to pace;
Or, o'er the stern reclining, watch below
The foaming wake far widening as we go.

On stormy nights when wild north-westers rave,
How proud a thing to fight with wind and wave!
The dripping sailor on the reeling mast
Exults to bear, and scorns to wish it past.

Where lies the land to which the ship would go?
Far, far ahead, is all her seaman know.
And where the land she travels from? Away,
Far, far behind, is all that they can say.

A.H. CLOUGH

DONKEY RIDING

Were you ever in Quebec,
Stowing timbers on a deck,
Where there's a king in his golden crown
   Riding on a donkey?

Hey ho, and away we go,
   Donkey riding, donkey riding,
Hey ho, and away we go,
   Riding on a donkey.

Were you ever in Cardiff Bay,
Where the folks all shout, Hooray!
Here comes John with his three months' pay,
   Riding on a donkey?

Hey ho, and away we go,
  Donkey riding, donkey riding,
Hey ho, and away we go,
  Riding on a donkey.

Were you ever off Cape Horn,
Where it's always fine and warm?
See the lion and the unicorn
  Riding on a donkey.

Hey ho, and away we go,
  Donkey riding, donkey riding,
Hey ho, and away we go,
  Riding on a donkey.

ANONYMOUS
ENGLISH SEA SHANTY

WYNKEN, BLYNKEN, AND NOD

Wynken, Blynken, and Nod one night
    Sailed off in a wooden shoe—
Sailed on a river of crystal light,
    Into a sea of dew.
"Where are you going, and what do you wish?"
    The old moon asked the three.
    "We have come to fish for the herring fish
    That live in this beautiful sea;
    Nets of silver and gold have we!"
        Said Wynken,
        Blynken,
        And Nod.

The old moon laughed and sang a song,
    As they rocked in the wooden shoe,
And the wind that sped them all night long
    Ruffled the waves of dew.
The little stars were the herring fish
    That lived in that beautiful sea—
    "Now cast your nets wherever you wish—
    Never afeard are we;"
So cried the stars to the fishermen three:

Wynken,
Blynken,
And Nod.

All night long their nets they threw
  To the stars in the twinkling foam—
Then down from the skies came the wooden shoe,
  Bringing the fishermen home;
'Twas all so pretty a sail it seemed
  As if it could not be,
And some folks thought 'twas a dream they'd dreamed
  Of sailing that beautiful sea—
  But I shall name you the fishermen three:
    Wynken,
    Blynken,
    And Nod.

Wynken and Blynken are two little eyes,
    And Nod is a little head,
And the wooden shoe that sailed the skies
    Is the wee one's trundle-bed.
So shut your eyes while mother sings
    Of wonderful sights that be,
And you shall see the beautiful things
    As you rock in the misty sea,
    Where the old shoe rocked the fishermen three:
        Wynken,
        Blynken,
        And Nod.

EUGENE FIELD

MY MOTHER SAID

My mother said, I never should
Play with gypsies in the wood.

If I did, then she would say:
"Naughty girl to disobey!

"Your hair shan't curl and your shoes shan't shine,
You gypsy girl, you shan't be mine!"

And my father said that if I did,
He'd rap my head with the teapot-lid.

My mother said that I never should
Play with the gypsies in the wood.

The wood was dark, the grass was green;
By came Sally with a tambourine.

I went to sea—no ship to get across;
I paid ten shillings for a blind white horse.

I upped on his back and was off in a crack,
Sally tell my mother I shall never come back.

ANONYMOUS
ENGLISH

THE JUMBLIES

They went to sea in a Sieve, they did,
  In a Sieve they went to sea;
In spite of all their friends could say,
On a winter's morn, on a stormy day,
  In a Sieve they went to sea!
And when the Sieve turned round and round,
And everyone cried, "You'll all be drowned!"
They called aloud, "Our Sieve ain't big,
But we don't care a button, we don't care a fig!
  In a Sieve we'll go to sea."
      Far and few, far and few,
        Are the lands where the Jumblies live;
        Their heads are green, and their hands are blue,
        And they went to sea in a Sieve.

They sailed away in a Sieve, they did,
  In a Sieve they sailed so fast;
With only a beautiful pea-green veil
Tied with a riband by way of a sail
  To a small tobacco-pipe mast;
And everyone said, who saw them go,
"O won't they be soon upset, you know,
For the sky is dark, and the voyage is long,

152

And happen what may, it's extremely wrong,
   In a Sieve to sail so fast."
      Far and few, far and few,
         Are the lands where the Jumblies live;
      Their heads are green, and their hands are blue,
         And they went to sea in a Sieve.

The water it soon came in, it did,
   The water is soon came in;
So to keep them dry, they wrapped their feet
In a pinky paper, all folded neat,
   And they fastened it down with a pin.
And they passed the night in a crockery jar,
And each of them said, "How wise we are!
Though the sky be dark and the voyage be long
Yet we never can think we were rash or wrong,
   While round in our Sieve we spin!"
      Far and few, far and few,
         Are the lands where the Jumblies live;
      Their heads are green, and their hands are blue,
         And they went to sea in a Sieve.

And all night long they sailed away;
   And when the sun went down,
They whistled and warbled a moony song,

To the echoing sound of a coppery gong,
  In the shade of the mountains brown.
"O Timballo! How happy we are,
When we live in a Sieve and a crockery jar,
And all night long in the moonlight pale,
We sail away with a pea-green sail
  In the shade of the mountains brown!"
      Far and few, far and few,
        Are the lands where the Jumblies live;
        Their heads are green, and their hands are blue,
        And they went to sea in a Sieve.

They sailed to the Western Sea, they did,
  To a land all covered with trees,
And they bought an Owl and a useful Cart,
And a pound of Rice and a Cranberry Tart,
  And a hive of silvery Bees.
And they bought a Pig, and some green Jack-daws,
And a lovely Monkey with lollipop paws,
And forty bottles of Ring-Bo-Ree,
  And no end of Stilton Cheese.
      Far and few, far and few,
        Are the lands where the Jumblies live;
        Their heads are green, and their hands are blue,
        And they went to sea in a Sieve.

And in twenty years they all came back,
  In twenty years or more.
And everyone said, "How tall they've grown!
For they've been to the Lakes, and the Torrible Zone,
  And the hills of the Chankly Bore;"
And they drank their health and gave them a feast
Of dumplings made of beautiful yeast;
And everyone said, "If we only live,
We, too, will go to sea in a Sieve—
  To the hills of the Chankly Bore!"
      Far and few, far and few,
        Are the lands where the Jumblies live;
        Their heads are green, and their hands are blue,
        And they went to sea in a Sieve.

EDWARD LEAR

155

THE BUTTERFLY'S BALL

Come take up your hats, and away let us haste,
To the Butterfly's Ball, and the Grasshopper's Feast.
The trumpeter Gadfly has summoned the crew,
And the revels are now only waiting for you.

On the smooth-shaven grass by the side of a wood,
Beneath a broad oak which for ages has stood,
See the children of earth and the tenants of air,
For an evening's amusement together repair.

And there came the Beetle, so blind and so black,
Who carried the Emmet, his friend, on his back.
And there came the Gnat, and the Dragonfly too,
And all their relations, green, orange, and blue.

And there came the Moth, with her plumage of down,
And the Hornet, with jacket of yellow and brown;
Who with him the Wasp, his companion, did bring,
But they promised that evening, to lay by their sting.

Then the sly little Dormouse crept out of his hole,
And led to the feast his blind cousin the Mole.
And the Snail, with his horns peeping out of his shell,
Came, fatigued with the distance, the length of an ell.

A mushroom their table, and on it was laid
A water-dock leaf, which a tablecloth made.
The viands were various, to each of their taste,
And the Bee brought the honey to sweeten the feast.

With steps most majestic the Snail did advance,
And he promised the gazers a minuet to dance;
But they all laughed so loud that he drew in his head,
And went in his own little chamber to bed.

Then, as evening gave way to the shadows of night,
Their watchman, the Glowworm, came out with his light.
So home let us hasten, while yet we can see;
For no watchman is waiting for you and for me.

WILLIAM ROSCOE

JABBERWOCKY

Tum Tum Tree
(BELLY BUTTON US
EXTRAORDINARIUS)

'Twas brillig, and the slithy toves
    Did gyre and gimble in the wabe:
All mimsy were the borogoves,
    And the mome raths outgrabe.

"Beware the Jabberwock, my son!
    The jaws that bite, the claws that catch!
Beware the Jubjub bird, and shun
    The frumious Bandersnatch!"

He took his vorpal sword in hand:
    Long time the manxome foe he sought—
So rested he by the Tumtum tree,
    And stood awhile in thought.

And as in uffish thought he stood,
    The Jabberwock, with eyes of flame,
Came whiffling through the tulgey wood,
    And burbled as it came!

One, two! One, two! And through and through
    The vorpal blade went snicker-snack!
He left it dead, and with its head
    He went galumphing back.

"And hast thou slain the Jabberwock?
    Come to my arms my beamish boy!
O frabjous day! Callooh! Callay!"
    He chortled in his joy.

'Twas brillig, and the slithy toves
    Did gyre and gimble in the wabe:
All mimsy were the borogoves,
    And the mome raths outgrabe.

LEWIS CARROLL

I SELL YOU THE KEY OF THE KING'S GARDEN

I sell you the key of the King's garden:

I sell you the string that ties the key of the King's garden:

I sell you the rat that gnawed the string that ties the key
of the King's garden:

I sell you the cat that caught the rat that gnawed the
string that ties the key of the King's garden:

I sell you the dog that bit the cat that caught the rat that
gnawed the string that ties the key of the King's garden.

ANONYMOUS
ENGLISH

160

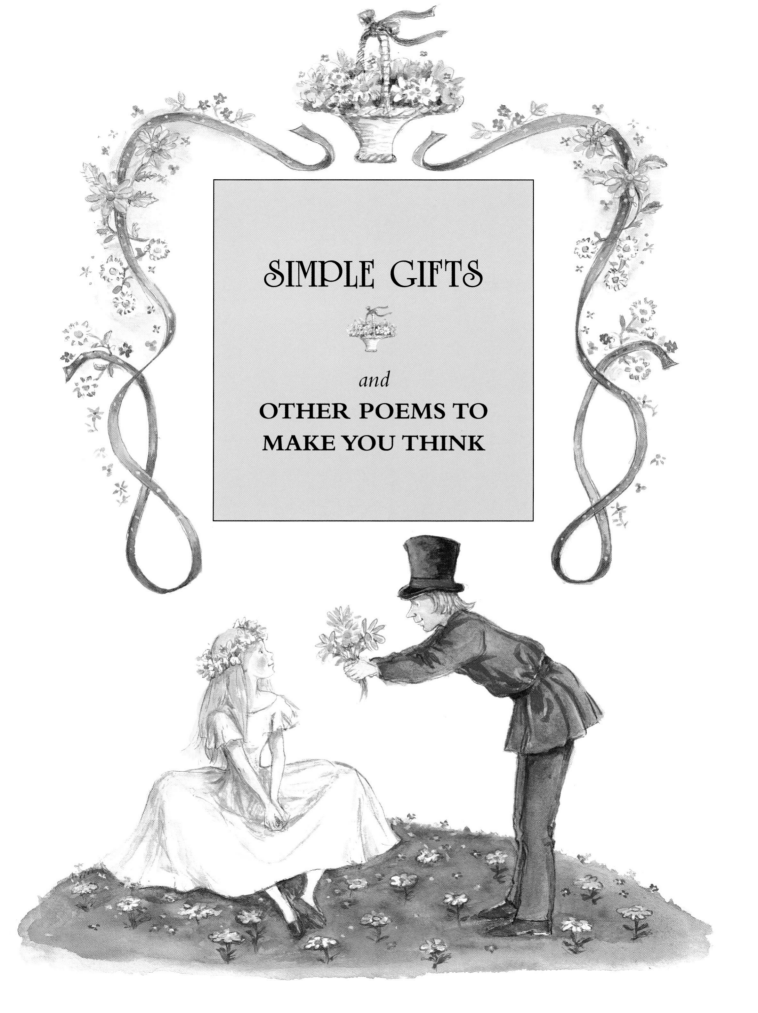

SIMPLE GIFTS

and

OTHER POEMS TO
MAKE YOU THINK

SIMPLE GIFTS

'Tis the gift to be simple,
'Tis the gift to be free,
'Tis the gift to come down
Where we ought to be,
And when we find ourselves
In the place just right,
'Twill be in the valley
Of love and delight.
When true simplicity is gained
To bow and to bend
We sha'n't be ashamed,
To turn, turn will be our delight,
Till by turning, turning
We come round right.

ANONYMOUS
AMERICAN, SHAKER SONG

LITTLE THINGS

Little drops of water,
  Little grains of sand,
Make the mighty ocean
  And the beauteous land.

And the little moments,
  Humble though they be,
Make the mighty ages
  Of eternity.

So our little errors
  Lead the soul away,
From the paths of virtue
  Into sin to stray.

Little deeds of kindness,
  Little words of love,
Make our earth an Eden,
  Like the heaven above.

JULIA A. CARNEY

WHOLE DUTY OF CHILDREN

A child should always say what's true,
And speak when he is spoken to,
And behave mannerly at table:
At least as far as he is able.

ROBERT LOUIS STEVENSON

DONT-CARE

Dont-care didn't care;
  Dont-care was wild.
Dont-care stole plum and pear
  Like any beggar's child.

Dont-care was made to care,
  Dont-care was hung:
Dont-care was put in the pot
  And boiled till he was done.

ANONYMOUS
ENGLISH

165

LOVING AND LIKING

There's more in words that I can teach:
Yet listen, Child—I would not preach,
But only give some plain directions
To guide your speech and your affections.

Say not you LOVE a roasted fowl,
But you may love a screaming owl
And, if you can, the unwieldy toad
That crawls from his secure abode
Within the mossy garden wall
When evening dews begin to fall.

And when, upon some showery day,
Into a path or public way
A frog leaps out from bordering grass,
Startling the timid as they pass,
Do you observe him, and endeavor
To take the intruder into favor,
Learning from him to find a reason
For a light heart in a dull season.

The spring's first rose by you espied

May fill your breast with joyful pride;

And you may love the strawberry-flower,

And love the strawberry in its bower;

But when the fruit, so often praised

For beauty, to your lip is raised,

Say not you LOVE the delicate treat,

But LIKE it, enjoy it, and thankfully eat.

Long may you love your pensioner mouse,

Though one of a tribe that torment the house:

Nor dislike her cruel sport the cat,

Deadly foe both of mouse and rat.

Remember she follows the law of her kind,

And Instinct is neither wayward nor blind.

Then think of her beautiful gliding form,

Her tread that would scarcely crush a worm,

And her soothing song by the winter fire,

Soft as the dying throb of the lyre.

I would not circumscribe your love:
It may soar with the eagle and brood with the dove,
May pierce the earth with the patient mole,
Or track the hedgehog to his hole.
Loving and liking are the solace of life,
Rock the cradle of joy, smooth the death-bed of strife.
You love your father and your mother,
Your grown-up and your baby brother:
You love your sister, and your friends,
And countless blessings, which God sends:
But LIKINGS come, and pass away:
'Tis love that remains till our latest day.

DOROTHY WORDSWORTH

PIPPA'S SONG

The year's at the spring,
And day's at the morn;
Morning's at seven;
The hillside's dew-pearl'd;
The lark's on the wing;
The snail's on the thorn;
God's in His heaven—
All's right with the world!

ROBERT BROWNING

AGAINST QUARRELING AND FIGHTING

Let dogs delight to bark and bite,
   For God hath made them so:
Let bears and lions growl and fight,
   For 'tis their nature, too.

But, children, you should never let
   Such angry passions rise:
Your little hands were never made
   To tear each other's eyes.

Let love through all your actions run,
   And all your words be mild:
Live like the blessed Virgin's Son,
   That sweet and lovely child.

His soul was gentle as a lamb;
    And as his nature grew,
He grew in favor both with man,
    And God his Father, too.

Now, Lord of all, he reigns above,
    And from his heavenly throne
He sees what children dwell in love,
    And marks them for his own.

ISAAC WATTS

THE WIND

Who has seen the wind?
　　Neither I nor you;
But when the leaves hang trembling
　　The wind is passing through.

Who has seen the wind?
　　Neither you nor I;
But when the trees bow down their heads
　　The wind is passing by.

CHRISTINA ROSSETTI

FROM A RAILWAY CARRIAGE

Faster than fairies, faster than witches,
Bridges and houses, hedges and ditches;
And charging along like troops in a battle,
All through the meadows the horses and cattle:
All of the sights of the hill and the plain
Fly as thick as driving rain;
And ever again, in the wink of an eye,
Painted stations whistle by.

Here is a child who clambers and scrambles,
All by himself and gathering brambles;
Here is a tramp who stands and gazes;
And there is the green for stringing the daisies!
Here is a cart run away in the road
Lumping along with man and load;
And here is a mill, and there is a river:
Each a glimpse and gone for ever!

ROBERT LOUIS STEVENSON

A BABY-SERMON

The lightning and thunder
They go and they come;
But the stars and the stillness
Are always at home.

GEORGE MACDONALD

WAGTAIL AND BABY

A baby watched a ford, whereto
  A wagtail came for drinking;
A blaring bull went wading through,
  The wagtail showed no shrinking.

A stallion splashed his way across,
  The birdie nearly sinking;
He gave his plumes a twitch and toss,
  And held his own unblinking.

Next saw the baby round the spot
  A mongrel slowing slinking;
The wagtail gazed, but faltered not
  In dip and sip and prinking.

A perfect gentleman then neared;
  The wagtail, in a winking,
With terror rose and disappeared;
  The baby fell a-thinking.

THOMAS HARDY

MY SHADOW

I have a little shadow that goes in and out with me,
And what can be the use of him is more than I can see.
He is very, very like me from the heels up to the head;
And I see him jump before me,
  when I jump into my bed.

The funniest thing about him is the way he likes to grow—
Not at all like proper children, which is always very slow;
For he sometimes shoots up taller like an india rubber ball,
And he sometimes gets so little that
  there's none of him at all.

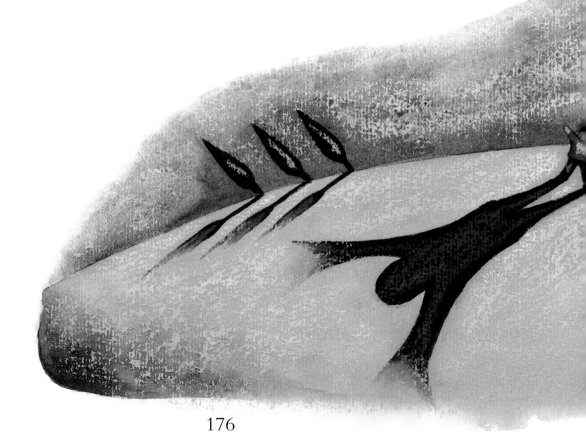

He hasn't got a notion of how children ought to play,
And can only make a fool of me in every sort of way.
He stays so close beside me, he's a coward you can see;
I'd think shame to stick to nursie
 as that shadow sticks to me!

One morning, very early, before the sun was up,
I rose and found the shining dew on every buttercup;
But my lazy little shadow, like an arrant sleepyhead,
Had stayed at home behind me and was
 fast asleep in bed.

ROBERT LOUIS STEVENSON

A CHRISTMAS CAROL

In the bleak midwinter
  Frosty wind made moan,
Earth stood hard as iron,
  Water like a stone;
Snow had fallen, snow on snow,
  Snow on snow,
In the bleak midwinter
  Long ago.

Our God, heaven cannot hold Him,
  Nor earth sustain;
Heaven and earth shall flee away
  When He comes to reign:
In the bleak midwinter
  A stable-place sufficed
The Lord God Almighty,
  Jesus Christ.

What can I give him,
  Poor as I am?
If I were a shepherd
  I would bring a lamb;
If I were a wise man
  I would do my part—
Yet what I can, I give Him,
  Give my heart.

CHRISTINA ROSSETTI

NOW THRICE WELCOME CHRISTMAS

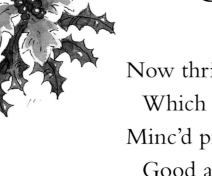

Now thrice welcome, Christmas,
  Which brings us good cheer,
Minc'd pies and plum porridge,
  Good ale and strong beer;
With pig, goose, and capon,
  The best that can be,
So well doth the weather
  And our stomachs agree.

Observe how the chimneys
  Do smoke all about,
The cooks are providing
  For dinner, no doubt;
For those on whose tables
  No victuals appear,
O may they keep Lent
  All the rest of the year!

With holly and ivy
So green and so gay,
We deck up our houses
As fresh as the day,
With bays and rosemary,
And laurel complete;
And every one now
Is a king in conceit.

ANONYMOUS
ENGLISH

CHRISTMAS BELLS

I heard the bells on Christmas Day
Their old familiar carols play,
    And wild and sweet
    The words repeat
Of Peace on earth, Goodwill to men!

And thought how, as the day had come,
The belfries of all Christendom
    Had rolled along
    The unbroken song
Of Peace on earth, Goodwill to men!

Till ringing, singing on its way,
The world revolved from night to day,
    A voice, a chime,
    A chant sublime,
Of Peace on earth, Goodwill to men!

Then from each black accursed mouth,
The cannon thundered in the South,
    And with the sound
    The carols drowned,
The Peace on earth, Goodwill to men!

And in despair I bowed my head;
"There is no peace on earth," I said,
   "For hate is strong
   And mocks the song
Of Peace on earth, Goodwill to men!"

Then peeled the bells more loud and deep:
"God is not dead, nor doth he sleep!
   The Wrong shall fail,
   The Right prevail,
With Peace on earth, Goodwill to men!"

HENRY WADSWORTH LONGFELLOW

THE OXEN

Christmas Eve, and twelve of the clock.
  "Now they are all on their knees,"
An elder said as we sat in a flock
  By the embers in hearthside ease.

We pictured the meek mild creatures where
  They dwelt in their strawy pen,
Nor did it occur to one of us there
  To doubt they were kneeling then.

So fair a fancy few would weave
   In these years! Yet, I feel,
If someone said on Christmas Eve,
   "Come; see the oxen kneel

"In the lonely barton by yonder coomb
   Our childhood used to know,"
I should go with him in the gloom,
   Hoping it might be so.

THOMAS HARDY

185

WHERE GO THE BOATS?

Dark brown is the river,
  Golden is the sand.
It flows along for ever,
  With trees on either hand.

Green leaves a-floating,
  Castles of the foam,
Boats of mine a-boating—
  Where will all come home?

On goes the river,
  And out past the mill,
Away down the valley,
  Away down the hill.

Away down the river,
  A hundred miles or more,
Other little children
  Shall bring my boats ashore.

ROBERT LOUIS STEVENSON

ARIEL'S SONG

Full fathom five thy father lies;
   Of his bones are coral made;
Those are pearls that were his eyes:
   Nothing of him that doth fade,
But doth suffer a sea-change
Into something rich and strange:
Sea nymphs hourly ring his knell.
   Ding-dong!
   Hark! now I hear them,
   Ding-dong, bell!

WILLIAM SHAKESPEARE

SPELLBOUND

The night is darkening round me,
The wild winds coldly blow;
But a tyrant spell has bound me
And I cannot, cannot go.

The giant trees are bending
Their bare boughs weighed with snow.
And the storm is fast descending,
And yet I cannot go.

Clouds beyond clouds above me,
Wastes beyond wastes below;
But nothing drear can move me;
I will not, cannot go.

EMILY BRONTË

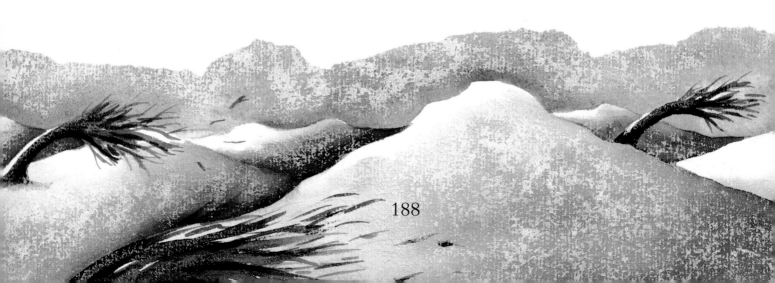

THE SHEPHERD BOY'S SONG

He that is down, needs fear no fall,
    He that is low, no pride;
He that is humble, ever shall
    Have God to be his guide.

I am content with what I have,
    Little be it, or much:
And, Lord, contentment still I crave,
    Because thou savest such.

Fullness to such a burden is
    That go on pilgrimage:
Here little, and hereafter bliss
    Is best from age to age.

JOHN BUNYAN

GOD BE IN MY HEAD

God be in my head
And in my Understanding.

God be in my eyes
And in my Looking.

God be in my mouth
And in my Speaking.

God be in my heart
And in my Thinking.

God be at mine end
And at my Departing.

ANONYMOUS
ENGLISH

THE OWL AND
THE PUSSY-CAT

and

OTHER STORY POEMS

THE OWL AND THE PUSSY-CAT

The Owl and the Pussy-Cat went to sea
   In a beautiful pea-green boat,
They took some honey, and plenty of money,
   Wrapped up in a five-pound note.
The Owl looked up to the stars above,
   And sang to a small guitar,
"O lovely Pussy! O Pussy, my love,
   What a beautiful Pussy you are,
       You are,
       You are,
   What a beautiful Pussy you are!"

Puss said to the Owl, "You elegant fowl!
   How charmingly sweet you sing!
O let us be married! too long we have tarried:
   But what shall we do for a ring?"
They sailed away for a year and a day,
   To the land where the Bong-tree grows,
And there in a wood a Piggy-wig stood,
   With a ring at the end of his nose,
       His nose,
       His nose,
   With a ring at the end of his nose.

"Dear Pig, are you willing to sell for one shilling,
Your ring?" Said the Piggy, "I will."
So they took it away, and were married next day
  By the Turkey who lived on the hill.
They dined on mince, and slices of quince,
  Which they ate with a runcible spoon:
And hand in hand, on the edge of the sand,
  They danced by the light of the moon,
        The moon,
        The moon,
They danced by the light of the moon.

EDWARD LEAR

THE DUEL

The gingham dog and the calico cat
    Side by side on the table sat;
'Twas half-past twelve, and (what do you think!)
Nor one nor t'other had slept a wink!
    The old Dutch clock and the Chinese plate
    Appeared to know as sure as fate
There was going to be a terrible spat.
    (I wasn't there; I simply state
    What was told to me by the Chinese plate!)

The gingham dog went "Bow-wow-wow!
And the calico cat replied "mee-ow!"
The air was littered, an hour or so,
With bits of gingham and calico,
    While the old Dutch clock in the chimney-place
    Up with its hands before its face,
For it always dreaded a family row!
    (Now mind: I'm only telling you
    What the old Dutch clock declares is true!)

Mee-ow

Bow-wow-wow

The Chinese plate looked very blue,
And wailed, "Oh, dear! what shall we do?"
But the gingham dog and the calico cat
Wallowed this way and tumbled that,
      Employing every tooth and claw
      In the awfullest way you ever saw—
And, oh! how the gingham and calico flew!
      (Don't fancy I exaggerate!
      I got my news from the Chinese plate!)

Next morning, where the two had sat,
They found no trace of dog or cat;
And some folks think unto this day
That burglars stole that pair away!
      But the truth about the cat and pup
      Is this: they ate each other up!
Now what do you really think of that!
      (The old Dutch clock it told me so,
      And that is how I came to know.)

EUGENE FIELD

FROG WENT A-COURTIN'

Mr Froggie went a-courtin' an' he did ride;
Sword and pistol by his side.

He went to Missus Mousie's hall,
Gave a loud knock and gave a loud call.

"Pray, Missus Mousie, air you within?"
"Yes, kind sir, I set an' spin."

He tuk Miss Mousie on his knee,
An' sez, "Miss Mousie, will ya marry me?"

Miss Mousie blushed an' hung her head,
"You'll have t'ask Uncle Rat," she said.

"Not without Uncle Rat's consent
Would I marry the Pres-i-dent."

Uncle Rat jumped up an' shuck his fat side,
To think his niece would be Bill Frog's bride.

Nex' day Uncle Rat went to town,
To git his niece a weddin' gown.

Whar shall the weddin' supper be?
'Way down yander in a holler tree.

First come in was a Bumble-bee,
Who danced a jig with Captain Flea.

Next come in was a Butterfly,
Sellin' butter very high.

An' when they all set down to sup,
A big gray goose come an' gobbled 'em all up.

An' this is the end of one, two, three,
The Rat an' the Mouse an' the little Froggie.

ANONYMOUS
AMERICAN

197

THE WALRUS AND THE CARPENTER

The sun was shining on the sea
  Shining with all his might:
He did his very best to make
  The billows smooth and bright—
And this was odd, because it was
  The middle of the night.

The moon was shining sulkily,
  Because she thought the sun
Had got no business to be there
  After the day was done—
"It's very rude of him," she said,
  "To come and spoil the fun!"

The sea was wet as wet could be,
  The sands were dry as dry.
You could not see a cloud, because
  No cloud was in the sky:
No birds were flying overhead—
  There were no birds to fly.

The Walrus and the Carpenter
  Were walking close at hand;
They wept like anything to see
  Such quantities of sand:
"If this were only cleared away,"
  They said, "it would be grand!"

"If seven maids with seven mops
  Swept it for half a year,
Do you suppose," the Walrus said,
  "That they could get it clear?"
"I doubt it," said the Carpenter,
  And shed a bitter tear.

"O Oysters, come and walk with us!"
  The Walrus did beseech.
"A pleasant walk, a pleasant talk,
  Along the briny beach:
We cannot do with more than four,
  To give a hand to each."

The eldest Oyster looked at him,
  But never a word he said:
The eldest Oyster winked his eye,
  And shook his heavy head—
Meaning to say he did not choose
  To leave the oyster-bed.

But four young Oysters hurried up,
  All eager for the treat:
Their coats were brushed, their faces washed,
  Their shoes were clean and neat—
And this was odd, because, you know,
  They hadn't any feet.

Four other Oysters followed them,
  And yet another four;
And thick and fast they came at last,
  And more, and more, and more—
All hopping through the frothy waves,
  And scrambling to the shore.

The Walrus and the Carpenter
  Walked on a mile or so,
And then they rested on a rock
  Conveniently low:
And all the little Oysters stood
  And waited in a row.

"The time has come," the Walrus said,
  "To talk of many things:
Of shoes—and ships—and sealing-wax—
  Of cabbages—and kings—
And why the sea is boiling hot—
  And whether pigs have wings."

"But wait a bit," the Oysters cried,
  "Before we have our chat;
For some of us are out of breath,
  And all of us are fat!"
"No hurry!" said the carpenter.
  They thanked him much for that.

"A load of bread," the Walrus said,
  "Is what we chiefly need:
Pepper and vinegar besides
  Are very good indeed—
Now if you're ready, Oysters dear,
  We can begin to feed."

"But not on us!" the Oysters cried,
  Turning a little blue.
"After such kindness, that would be
  A dismal thing to do!"
"The night is fine," the Walrus said,
  "Do you admire the view?

"It was so kind of you to come!
  And you are very nice!"
The Carpenter said nothing but
  "Cut us another slice:
I wish you were not quite so deaf—
  I've had to ask you twice!"

"It seems a shame," the Walrus said,
  "To play them such a trick,
After we've brought them out so far,
  And made them trot so quick!"
The Carpenter said nothing but
  "The butter's spread too thick!"

"I weep for you," the Walrus said:
  "I deeply sympathize."
With sobs and tears he sorted out
  Those of the largest size,
Holding his pocket-handkerchief
  Before his streaming eyes.

"O Oysters," said the Carpenter,
  "You've had a pleasant run!
Shall we be trotting home again?"
  But answer cam there none—
And this was scarcely odd, because
  They'd eaten every one.

LEWIS CARROLL

ELDORADO

Gaily bedight
A gallant knight,
In sunshine and in shadow,
Had journeyed long,
Singing a song,
In search of Eldorado.

But he grew old—
This knight so bold—
And o'er his heart a shadow
Fell as he found
No spot of ground
That looked like Eldorado.

And, as his strength
Failed him at length,
He met a pilgrim shadow:
"Shadow," said he,
"Where can it be,
This land of Eldorado?"

"Over the mountains
    Of the Moon,
Down the valley of the Shadow,
    Ride, boldly ride,"
    The shade replied,
"If you seek for Eldorado."

EDGAR ALLAN POE

THERE'S A HOLE IN THE MIDDLE
OF THE SEA

There's a hole, there's a hole,
  there's a hole in the middle of the sea.

There's a log in the hole in the middle of the sea.

There's a hole, there's a hole,
  there's a hole in the middle of the sea.

There's a bump on the log in the
  hole in the middle of the sea.

There's a hole, there's a hole,
  there's a hole in the middle of the sea.

There's a frog on the bump on the log
  in the hole in the middle of the sea.

There's a hole, there's a hole,
  there's a hole in the middle of the sea.

There's a fly on the frog on the bump
   on the log in the hole in the middle of the sea.

There's a hole, there's a hole,
   there's a hole in the middle of the sea.

There's a wing on the fly on the frog on the
   bump on the log in the hole in the middle of the sea.

There's a hole, there's a hole,
   there's a hole in the middle of the sea.

There's a flea on the wing on the fly
   on the frog on the bump on the log in the
   hole in the middle of the sea.

There's a hole, there's a hole,
   there's a hole in the middle of the sea.

ANONYMOUS
AMERICAN

THE WAR SONG OF DINAS VAWR

The mountain sheep are sweeter,
But the valley sheep are fatter;
We therefore deemed it meeter
To carry off the latter.
We made an expedition;
We met a host and quelled it;
We forced a strong position,
And killed the men who held it.

On Dyfed's richest valley.
Where herds of kine were browsing,
We made a mighty sally,
To furnish our carousing.
Fierce warriors rushed to meet us;
We met them and o'erthrew them:
They struggled hard to beat us;
But we conquered them, and slew them.

As we drove out prize at leisure,
The king marched forth to catch us;
His rage surpassed all measure,
But his people could not match us.
He fled to his hall pillars;

And, ere our force we led off,
Some sacked his house and cellars,
While others cut his head off.

We there, in strife bewildering,
Spilt blood enough to swim in:
We orphaned many children,
And widowed many women.
The eagles and the ravens
We glutted with our foemen:
The heroes and the cravens,
The spearmen and the bowmen.

We brought away from battle,
And much their land bemoaned them,
Two thousand head of cattle,
And the head of him who owned them:
Edynfed, King of Dyfed,
His head was borne before us;
His wine and beasts supplied our feasts,
And his overthrow, our chorus,

THOMAS LOVE PEACOCK

HUMPTY DUMPTY'S POEM

In winter, when the fields are white,
I sing this song for your delight—

In spring, when woods are getting green,
I'll try and tell you what I mean.

In summer, when the days are long,
Perhaps you'll understand the song:

In autumn, when the leaves are brown,
Take pen and ink, and write it down.

I sent a message to the fish:
I told them "This is what I wish."

The little fishes of the sea,
They sent an answer back to me.

The little fishes' answer was
"We cannot do it, Sir, because—"

I sent to them again to say
"It will be better to obey."

The fishes answered with a grin,
"Why, what a temper you are in!"

I told them once, I told them twice:
They would not listen to advice.

I took a kettle large and new,
Fit for the deed I had to do.

My heart went hop, my heart went thump;
I filled the kettle at the pump.

Then someone came to me and said,
"The little fishes are in bed."

I said to him, I said it plain,
"Then you must wake them up again."

I said it very loud and clear;
I went and shouted in his ear.

But he was very stiff and proud;
He said "You needn't shout so loud!"

And he was very proud and stiff;
He said "I'd go and wake them, if—"

I took a corkscrew from the shelf:
I went to wake them up myself.

And when I found the door was locked,
I pulled and pushed and kicked and knocked.

And when I found the door was shut,
I tried to turn the handle, but—

LEWIS CARROLL

A VISIT FROM ST. NICHOLAS

'Twas the night before Christmas, when all through the house

Not a creature was stirring, not even a mouse;

The stockings were hung by the chimney with care,

In hopes that St. Nicholas soon would be there;

The children were nestled all snug in their beds,

While visions of sugar-plums danced in their heads;

And Mamma in her 'kerchief and I in my cap,

Had just settled our brains for a long winter's nap—

When out on the lawn there arose such a clatter,

I sprang from my bed to see what was the matter.

Away to the window I flew like a flash,

Tore open the shutters, and threw up the sash.

The moon, on the breast of the new-fallen snow,

Gave the lustre of midday to objects below;

When, what to my wondering eyes should appear,

But a miniature sleigh and eight tiny reindeer,

With a little old driver, so lively and quick,

I knew in a moment it must be St. Nick.

More rapid than eagles his coursers they came,
And he whistled, and shouted, and called them by name:
"Now, *Dasher*! now, *Dancer*! now, *Prancer* and *Vixen*!
On, *Comet*! on, *Cupid*! on, *Donder* and *Blitzen*!
To the top of the porch! to the top of the wall!
Now dash away! dash away! dash away all!"

As dry leaves that before the wild hurricane fly,
When they meet with an obstacle, mount to the sky;
So up to the house-top the coursers they flew
With the sleigh full of toys, and St. Nicholas too.
And then, in a twinkling, I heard on the roof
The prancing and pawing of each little hoof—
As I drew in my head, and was turning around,
Down the chimney St. Nicholas came with a bound.

He was dressed all in fur, from his head to his foot,
And his clothes were all tarnished with ashes and soot;
A bundle of toys he had flung on his back,
And he looked like a pedlar just opening his pack.
His eyes—how they twinkled; his dimples, how merry!
His cheeks were like roses, his nose like a cherry!
His droll little mouth was drawn up like a bow,
And the beard of his chin was as white as the snow;
The stump of a pipe he held tight in his teeth,
And the smoke it encircled his head like a wreath;
He had a broad face and a little round belly
That shook, when he laughed, like a bowl full of jelly.
He was chubby and plump, a right jolly old elf,
And I laughed when I saw him, in spite of myself;

A wink of his eye and a twist of his head
Soon gave me to know I had nothing to dread;
He spoke not a word, but went straight to his work,
And filled all the stockings; then turned with a jerk,
And laying his finger aside of his nose,
And giving a nod, up the chimney he rose;
He sprang to his sleigh, to his team gave a whistle,
And away they all flew like the down of a thistle.
But I heard him exclaim, ere he drove out of sight,
"Happy Christmas to all, and to all a good night!"

CLEMENT CLARKE MOORE

ROLL OVER

There were ten in the bed
And the little one said:
  "Roll over! Roll over!"
So they all rolled over,
And one fell out.

There were nine in the bed
And the little one said:
  "Roll over! Roll over!"
So they all rolled over,
And one fell out.

There were eight in the bed
And the little one said:
  "Roll over, Roll over!"
So they all rolled over
And one fell out.

There were seven in the bed
And the little one said:
  "Roll over, Roll over!"
So they all rolled over,
And one fell out.

There were six in the bed
And the little one said;
  "Roll over! Roll over!"
So they all rolled over,
And one fell out.

There were five in the bed
And the little one said:
   "Roll over! Roll over!"
So they all rolled over,
And one fell out.

There were four in the bed
And the little one said:
  "Roll over! Roll over!"
So they all rolled over,
And one fell out.

There were three in the bed
And the little one said:
  "Roll over! Roll over!"
So they all rolled over,
And one fell out.

There were two in the bed
And the little one said:
 "Roll over! Roll over!"
So they all rolled over,
And one fell out.

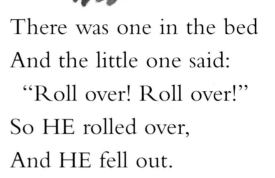

There was one in the bed
And the little one said:
 "Roll over! Roll over!"
So HE rolled over,
And HE fell out.

So there was the bed—
And no one said:
 "Roll over! Roll over!"

ANONYMOUS
ENGLISH

220

HUSH LITTLE BABY

and

OTHER BEDTIME POEMS

HUSH, LITTLE BABY

Hush, little baby, don't say a word,
Papa's going to buy you a mocking bird.

If the mocking bird won't sing,
Papa's going to buy you a diamond ring.

If the diamond ring turn to brass,
Papa's going to buy you a looking-glass.

If the looking-glass gets broke,
Papa's going to buy you a billy-goat.

If that billy-goat runs away,
Papa's going to buy you another today.

ANONYMOUS
AMERICAN

222

THE MOUSE'S LULLABY

Oh, rock–a–by, baby mouse, rock–a–by, so!
When baby's asleep to the baker's I'll go,
And while he's not looking I'll pop from a hole,
And bring to my baby a fresh penny roll.

PALMER COX

223

IN THE TREE-TOP

"Rock-a-by, baby, up in the tree-top!"
  Mother his blanket is spinning;
And a light little rustle that never will stop,
  Breezes and boughs are beginning.
Rock-a-by, baby, swinging so high!
        Rock-a-by!

"When the wind blows, then the cradle will rock."
  Hush! now it stirs in the bushes;
Now with a whisper, a flutter of talk,
  Baby and hammock it pushes.
Rock-a-by, baby! shut, pretty eye!
        Rock-a-by!

"Rock with the boughs, rock-a-by, baby dear!"
  Leaf-tongues are singing and saying;
Mother she listens, and sister is near,
  Under the tree softly playing.
Rock-a-by, baby! mother's close by!
        Rock-a-by!

Weave him a beautiful dream, little breeze!
Little leaves, nestle around him!
He will remember the song of the trees,
When age with silver has crowned him.
Rock-a-by, baby! wake by-and-by!
Rock-a-by!

Lucy Larcom

A CRADLE SONG

Golden slumbers kiss your eyes,
Smiles awake you when you rise.
Sleep, pretty wantons, do not cry,
And I will sing a lullaby:
Rock them, rock them, lullaby.

Care is heavy, therefore sleep you;
You are care, and care must keep you.
Sleep, pretty wantons, do not cry,
And I will sing a lullaby:
Rock them, rock them, lullaby.

THOMAS DEKKER

A CHILD'S EVENING PRAYER

Ere on my bed my limbs I lay,

God grant me grace my prayers to say:

O God, preserve my mother dear

In strength and health for many a year;

And, O! preserve my father too,

And may I pay him reverence due;

And may I my best thoughts employ

To be my parents' hope and joy;

And O! preserve my brothers both

From evil doings and from sloth,

And may we always love each other

Our friends, out father, and our mother:

And still, O Lord, to me impart

An innocent and grateful heart,

That after my great sleep I may

Awake to thy eternal day! Amen.

SAMUEL TAYLOR COLERIDGE

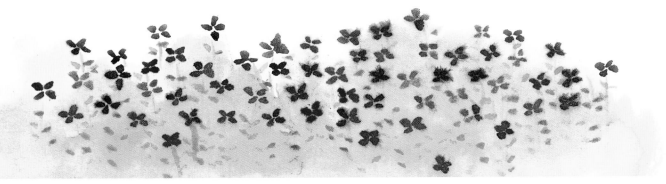

227

SONG OF THE SKY LOOM

O our Mother the Earth, O our Father the Sky,
Your children are we, and with tired backs
We bring you the gifts that you love.
Then weave for us a garment of brightness;
May the warp be the white light of morning,
May the weft be the red light of evening,
May the fringes be the falling rain,
May the border be the standing rainbow.
Thus weave for us a garment of brightness,
That we may walk fittingly where birds sing,
That we way walk fittingly where grass is green,
O our Mother the Earth, O our Father the sky.

ANONYMOUS
NATIVE AMERICAN, TEWA

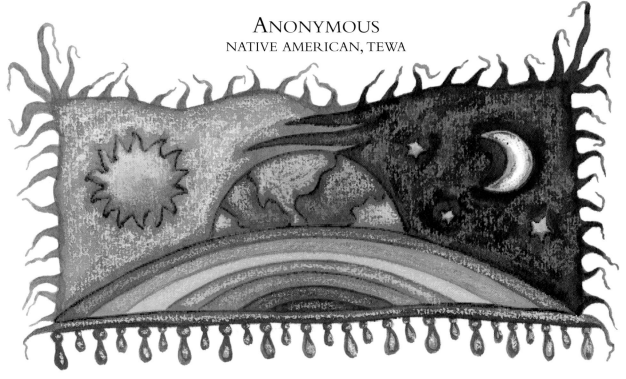

PUTTING THE WORLD TO BED

The little snow people are hurrying down
   From their home in the clouds overhead;
They are working as hard as ever they can,
   Putting the world to bed.

Every tree in a soft fleecy nightgown they clothe;
   Each part has its night-cap of white.
And o'er the cold ground a thick cover they spread
   Before they say good night.

And so they come eagerly sliding down,
   With a swift and silent tread,
Always as busy as busy can be,
   Putting the world to bed.

ESTHER W. BUXTON

NOW THE DAY IS OVER

Now the day is over,
  Night is drawing nigh,
Shadows of the evening
  Steal across the sky.

Now the darkness gathers,
  Stars begin to peep,
Birds and beasts and flowers
  Soon will be asleep.

Jesu, give the weary
  Calm and sweet repose;
With thy tenderest blessing
  May our eyelids close.

Grant to little children
  Visions bright of thee;
Guard the sailors tossing
  On the deep blue sea.

Comfort every sufferer
  Watching late in pain;
Those who plan some evil
  From their sin restrain.

Through the long night-watches
  May thine angels spread
Their white wings above me,
  Watching round my bed.

When the morning wakens,
  Then may I arise
Pure and fresh and sinless
  In thy holy eyes.

Glory to he Father,
  Glory to the son,
And to thee, blest Spirit,
  Whilst all ages run.

SABINE BARING-GOULD

EVENING

(In words of one syllable)

The day is past, the sun is set,
   And the white stars are in the sky;
While the long grass with dew is wet,
   And through the air the bats now fly.

The lambs have now lain down to sleep,
   The birds have long since sought their nests,
The air is still, and dark, and deep
   On the hill side the old wood rests.

Yet of the dark I have no fear,
   But feel as safe as when 'tis light;
For I know God is with me there,
   And He will guard me through the night.

For God is by me when I pray,
   And when I close mine eyes in sleep,
I know that He will with me stay,
   And will all night watch by me keep.

For He who rules the stars and sea,
  Who makes the grass and trees to grow,
Will look on a poor child like me,
  When on my knees I to Him bow.

He holds all things in His right hand,
  The rich, the poor, the great, the small;
When we sleep, or sit, or stand,
  Is with us, for He loves us all.

THOMAS MILLER

NIGHT

The sun descending in the west,
The evening star does shine;
The birds are silent in their nest,
And I must seek for mine.
    The moon, like a flower,
    In heaven's high bower,
    With silent delight
    Sits and smiles on the night.

Farewell, green fields and happy groves,
Where flocks have took delight;
Where lambs have nibbled, silent moves
The feet of angels bright;
    Unseen they pour blessing,
    And joy without ceasing,
    On each bud and blossom,
    And each sleeping bosom.

They look in every thoughtless nest,
Where birds are covered warm;
They visit caves of every beast,
To keep them all from harm.
  If they see any weeping,
  That should have been sleeping,
  They pour sleep on their head,
  And sit down by their bed.

When wolves and tigers howl for prey,
They pitying stand and weep;
Seeking to drive their thirst away,
And keep them from the sheep.
  But if they rush dreadful,
  The angels, most heedful,
  Receive each mild spirit,
  New worlds to inherit.

And there the lion's ruddy eyes
Shall flow with tears of gold,
And pitying the tender cries,
And walking round the fold,
　　Saying, "Wrath, by his meekness,
　　And, by his health, sickness
　　Is driven away
　　From our immortal day.

"And now beside thee, bleating lamb,
I can lie down and sleep;
Or think on him who bore thy name,
Graze after thee and weep.
　　For, washed in life's river,
　　My bright mane for ever
　　Shall shine like the gold,
　　As I guard o'er the fold."

WILLIAM BLAKE

BED IN SUMMER

In winter I get up at night
And dress by yellow candlelight.
In summer, quite the other way,
I have to go to bed by day.

I have to go to bed and see
The birds still hopping on the tree,
Or hear the grown-up people's feet
Still going past me in the street.

And does it not seem hard to you,
When all the sky is clear and blue,
And I should like so much to play,
To have to go to bed by day?

ROBERT LOUIS STEVENSON

NIGHT SOUNDS

Midnight's bell goes ting, ting, ting, ting, ting,

Then dogs do howl, and not a bird does sing

But the nightingale, and she cries twit, twit, twit;

Owls then on every bough do sit;

Ravens croak on chimneys' tops;

The cricket in the chamber hops;

The nibbling mouse is not asleep,

But he goes peep, peep, peep, peep, peep;

  And the cats cry mew, mew, mew,

  And still the cats cry mew, mew, mew.

THOMAS MIDDLETON

SWEET AND LOW

Sweet and low, sweet and low,
    Wind of the western sea,
Low, low, breathe and blow,
    Wind of the western sea!
Over the rolling waters go,
Come from the dying moon, and blow,
    Blow him again to me;
While my little one, while my pretty one, sleeps.

Sleep and rest, sleep and rest,
    Father will come to thee soon;
Rest, rest, on mother's breast,
    Father will come to thee soon;
Father will come to his babe in the nest,
Silver sails all out of the west
    Under the silver moon:
Sleep, my little one, sleep, my pretty one, sleep.

ALFRED, LORD TENNYSON

DREAMS

Beyond, beyond the mountain line,
　The grey-stone and the boulder,
Beyond the growth of dark green pine,
　That crowns its western shoulder,
There lies that fairy land of mine,
　Unseen of a beholder.

Its fruits are all like rubies rare,
　Its streams are clear as glasses:
There golden castles hang in air,
　And purple grapes in masses,
And noble knights and ladies fair
　Come riding down the passes.

Ah me! they say if I could stand
　Upon those mountain ledges,
I should but see on either hand
　Plain fields and dusty hedges:
And yet I know my fairy land
　Lies somewhere o'er their hedges.

CECIL FRANCES ALEXANDER

DREAMS

Here we are all, by day; by night we are hurled
By dreams, each one into a several world.

ROBERT HERRICK

THE SUGAR-PLUM TREE

Have you ever heard of the Sugar-Plum Tree?
  'Tis a marvel of great renown!
It blooms on the shore of the Lollipop sea
  In the garden of Shut-Eye Town:
The fruit that it bears is so wondrously sweet
  (As those who have tasted it say)
That good little children have only to eat
  Of that fruit to be happy next day.

When you've got to the tree, you would have a hard time
  To capture the fruit which I sing;
The tree is so tall that no person could climb
  To the boughs where the sugar-plums swing.
But up in that tree sits a chocolate cat,
  And a gingerbread dog prowls below—
And this is the way you contrive to get at
  Those sugar-plums tempting you so:

You say but the word to that gingerbread dog
  And he barks with such terrible zest
That the chocolate cat is at once all agog,
  As her swelling proportions attest.
And the chocolate cat goes cavorting around
  From this leafy limb unto that,
And the sugar-plums tumble, of course, to the ground—
  Hurrah for that chocolate cat!

There are marshmallows, gumdrops, and peppermint canes,
  With striplings of scarlet or gold,
And you carry away of the treasure that rains
  As much as your apron can hold!
So come, little child, cuddle closer to me
  In your dainty white nightcap and gown,
And I'll rock you away to that Sugar-Plum Tree
  In the garden of Shut-Eye Town.

EUGENE FIELD

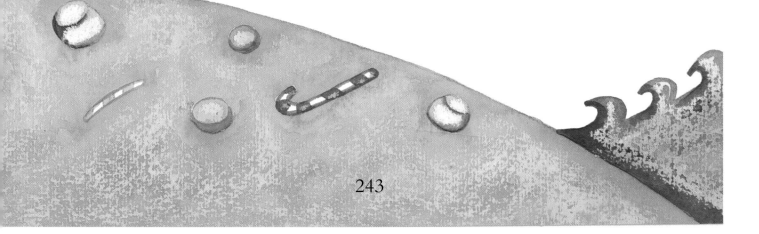

LADY MOON

Lady Moon, Lady Moon, where are you roving?
    Over the sea.
Lady Moon, Lady Moon, whom are you loving?
    All that love me.

Are you not tired with rolling, and never
    Resting to sleep?
Why look so pale, and so sad, as for ever
    Wishing to weep?

Ask me not this, little child, if you love me;
    You are too bold;
I must obey my dear Father above me,
    And do as I'm told.

Lady Moon, Lady Moon, where are you roving?
    Over the sea.
Lady Moon, Lady Moon, whom are you loving?
    All that love me.

RICHARD MONCKTON MILNES, LORD HOUGHTON

THE MOON

The moon has a face like the clock in the hall;
She shines on thieves on the garden wall,
On streets and fields and harbour quays,
And birdies asleep in the forks of the trees.

The squalling cat and the squeaking mouse,
The howling dog by the door of the house,
The bat that lies in bed at noon,
All love to be out by the light of the moon.

But all of the things that belong to the day
Cuddle to sleep to be out of her way;
And flowers and children close their eyes
Till up in the morning the sun shall arise.

ROBERT LOUIS STEVENSON

THE STAR

Twinkle, twinkle, little star,
How I wonder what you are!
Up above the world so high,
Like a diamond in the sky.

When the blazing sun is gone,
When he nothing shines upon,
Then you show your little light,
Twinkle, twinkle, all the night.

Then the traveller in the dark,
Thanks you for your tiny spark,
He could not see which way to go,
If you did not twinkle so.

In the dark blue sky you keep,
And often through my curtains peep,
For you never shut your eye,
Till the sun is in the sky.

As your bright and tiny spark,
Lights the traveller in the dark—
Though I know not what you are,
Twinkle, twinkle, little star.

JANE TAYLOR

LADY MOON

O Lady Moon, your horns point toward the east:
    Shine, be increased.
O Lady Moon, your horns point toward the west:
    Wane, be at rest.

CHRISTINA ROSSETTI

THE SONG OF THE STARS

We are the stars which sing,
We sing with our light.
We are the birds of fire
We fly over the sky,
Our light is a voice.
We make a road for spirits,
For the spirits to pass over.

Among us are three hunters
Who chase a bear;
There never was a time
When they were not hunting.
We look down on the mountains.
This is the song of the stars.

ANONYMOUS
NATIVE AMERICAN, PASSAMAQUODDY

LIE A-BED

Lie a-bed,
Sleepy head,
Shut up eyes, bo-peep;
Till daybreak
Never wake:—
Baby, sleep.

CHRISTINA ROSSETTI

INDEX OF TITLES
AND FIRST LINES

Titles are set in *italic*. Where the title and the first line are the same, the first line only is listed.

SMALL IS THE WREN

Small is the wren,
 Black is the rook,
Great is the sinner
 That steals this book.